Glasgow

DIAMOND BOOKS

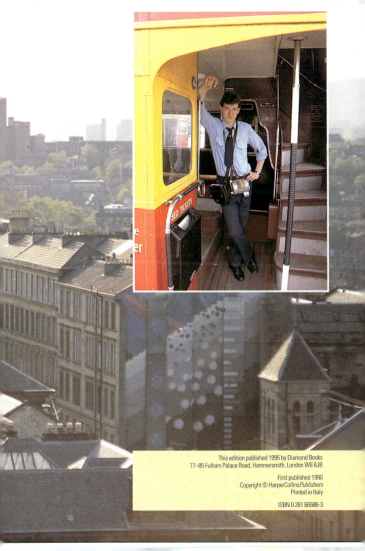

This edition published 1995 by Diamond Books
77–85 Fulham Palace Road, Hammersmith, London W6 8JB

First published 1990
Copyright © HarperCollins Publishers
Printed in Italy

ISBN 0 261 66586-3

HOW TO USE THIS BOOK

The blue-coded 'topic' section answers the question 'I would like to see or do something; where do I go and what do I see when I get there?' A simple, clear layout provides an alphabetical list of activities and events, offers you a selection of each, tells you how to get there, what it will cost, when it is open and what to expect. Each topic in the list has its own simplified map, showing the position of each item and the nearest landmark or transport access, for instant orientation. Whether your interest is Architecture or Sport you can find all the information you need quickly and simply. Where major resorts within an area require in-depth treatment, they follow the main topics section in alphabetical order.

The red-coded section is a lively and informative gazetteer. In one alphabetical list you can find essential facts about the main places and cultural items - 'What is La Bastille?', 'Who was Michelangelo?' - as well as practical and invaluable travel information. It covers everything you need to know to help you enjoy yourself and get the most out of your time away, from Accommodation through Babysitters, Car Hire, Food, Health, Money, Newspapers, Taxis and Telephones to Zoos.

Cross-references: Type in small capitals - CHURCHES - tells you that more information on an item is available within the topic on churches. A-Z in bold - **A-Z** - tells you that more information is available on an item within the gazetteer. Simply look under the appropriate heading. A name in bold - **Holy Cathedral** - also tells you that more information on an item is available in the gazetteer under that particular heading.

Photographs by **Phil Springthorpe**
Cover picture by **James Carney**

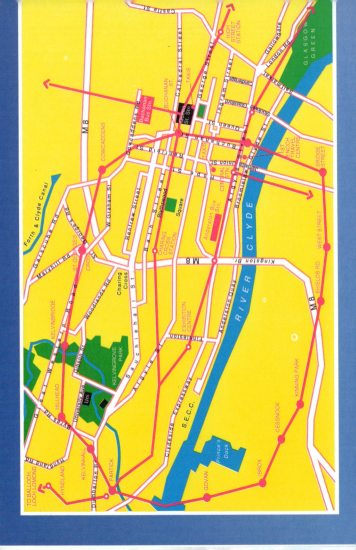

INTRODUCTION

Visitors to the city may be surprised to discover that instead of a grim and forbidding place plagued by economic stagnation, crime and social deprivation, Glasgow is a lively, attractive, cosmopolitan and friendly city, with plenty to do and see. In the past Glasgow may have partly deserved its unsavoury reputation - the legacy of industrial decline after the war - but in the last 15 years much has happened to dispel this negative image and to improve the fortunes of the city and its people. Glasgow in the 1990s is definitely 'miles better' and a desirable location for tourists to visit and explore.

The history of pre-medieval Glasgow is obscured by legend and difficult to trace - according to tradition, the city's origins lie in the 6th century with the foundation of a religious community by St Mungo on the banks of the Molendinar Burn, a tributary of the Clyde. The erection of the cathedral over the tomb of St Mungo in 1136 by Bishop Achaius, and the foundation of the university in 1451 by Bishop Turnbull confirmed medieval Glasgow as a centre of religion and learning. Although commerce supplanted clericalism during the 17th century, it was greater access to trade with the colonies after the Act of Union with England in 1707, which, by mid-century, transformed Glasgow into a prosperous commercial town, dominated by the Tobacco Lords - a merchant elite enriched by the importing of tobacco and cotton from North America. Later, during the Industrial Revolution, Glasgow established itself as a leading manufacturer of textiles, chemicals, iron and steel, and by the late 1880s as the world centre of shipbuilding and heavy engineering - the 'Second City of the Empire'. The erosion of the city's industrial pre-eminence during the 1920s and 30s accelerated after the war, causing massive unemployment and social hardship. It was during this period that the city acquired its reputation as a grim, hard-drinking and violent slum. This image, however, was often exaggerated by outsiders, and even, to a certain extent, by Glaswegians themselves - brandished as a peverse symbol of superiority to the inhabitants of other, less unfortunate, cities. At the same time, this image ignored the essential warm-heartedness, humour and resilience of Glaswegians in facing the hardships of post-industrialism and government neglect.

Glasgow today is certainly much improved, although problems like bad housing and unemployment remain in some areas. This improvement is

strikingly manifested in the appearance of the city itself. An extensive programme of renovation and stone cleaning has rescued the Victorian city from decades of soot and grime. Buildings like the City Chambers stand revealed as impressive memorials to the pride and prosperity of the Victorian era. A major new building programme has added hotels and conference facilities; an exhibition centre; new shopping precincts such as Princes Square and the St Enoch Centre; and a new concert hall (due to open in 1990). Much of the centre has become pedestrianized, ideal for street entertainers and shoppers alike. East of George Square, the Merchant City has been refurbished, with old warehouses and buildings converted into smart residences, shops, bars and cafés.

As well as the physical changes to the city enviroment, there has been a revival of pride and hope for the future, embodied in recent achievements in the arts. Glasgow's nomination as European City of Culture 1990 is regarded as a fitting tribute to the city which hosts the Mayfest (an international festival of music, drama, and comedy) and the International Jazz Festival; is the home of Scottish Opera and Ballet, the Royal Scottish Academy of Music and Drama and the famous Citizens' Theatre; boasts outstanding museums such as the Burrell Collection and Kelvingrove Art Gallery (as well as numerous small independent galleries); and has produced novelists and film makers like Alasdair Gray and Bill Forsyth. An impressive series of events will take place in 1990, in all branches of the arts, and various special events are also planned, such as the return of great Clyde-built vessels - like the QE2 - to the city of their birth.

These cultural facilities are only one facet of the city's attractions; it also has over 70 public parks, including Glasgow Green, which is also the site of the People's Palace Museum devoted to the social and economic history of the city; Pollok Park, site of the Burrell; and Kelvingrove Park and the Botanic Gardens in the west end. The city also contains a fine selection of bars and restaurants to suit all tastes, as well as cinemas, nightclubs, discos and live music venues. Last but not least, Glasgow is also an ideal base for exploring the Scottish countryside: unquestionably the most beautiful and dramatic in the British Isles. Twenty years ago, the prospect of Glasgow as a tourist centre would have been greeted with ridicule; today that prospect is fast becoming a reality, and is greeted with enthusiasm by the city and its people.

Callum Brines

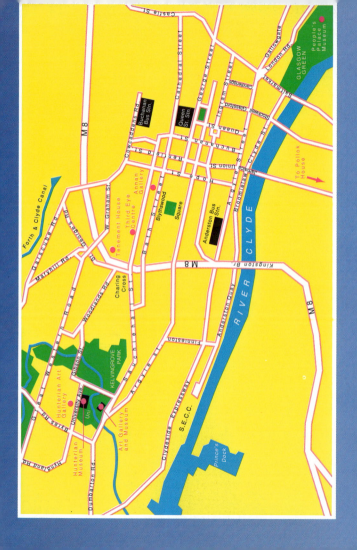

KELVINGROVE ART GALLERY AND MUSEUM Argyle St.
•1000-1700 Mon.-Sat., 1400-1700 Sun. ∪ Kelvinhall. •Free.
The finest civic art collection outside London. See **WALK 3**, **A-Z**.

HUNTERIAN ART GALLERY Glasgow University, 82 Hillhead St.
•0930-1700 Mon.-Fri., 0930-1300 Sat. ∪ Hillhead. •Free.
*European art, British portraiture, Scottish works, a reconstruction of
Mackintosh's house, and the outstanding Whistler Collection.
See* **MACKINTOSH**.

THE HUNTERIAN MUSEUM Glasgow University, University Av.
•0930-1700 Mon.-Fri., Sat. 0930-1300. ∪ Hillhead. •Free.
*Geological, archaeological and other items based on the bequest of William
Hunter (1718-83), including his superb Coin Collection. See* **WALK 3**.

THE PEOPLE'S PALACE MUSEUM Glasgow Green.
•1000-1700 Mon.-Sat., 1400-1700 Sun. •Free.
Exhibits reflecting the social and economic history of Glasgow. See **A-Z**.

POLLOK HOUSE Pollok Country Park, 2060 Pollokshaws Rd.
•1000-1700 Mon.-Sat., 1400-1700 Sun. Beside the Burrell. •Free.
*18thC mansion with furniture, ceramics, silver and glassware, and superb
paintings including works by El Greco, Murillo, and Blake.*

THE TENEMENT HOUSE 145 Buccleuch St.
•1400-1600 Sat., Sun. (Jan.-Easter); 1400-1700 daily (Easter-31 Oct.).
∪ Cowcaddens. •£1, child 50p.
Recreation of a typical late-19thC Glasgow family home. See **WALK 2**, **A-Z**.

THIRD EYE CENTRE 350 Sauchiehall St.
•0100-1730 Tues.-Sat., 1400-1730 Sun. Near Charing Cross. •Free.
Showcase for the contemporary arts, with a bookshop and wholefood café.

ANNAN GALLERY 130 West Campbell St.
•0900-1700 Mon.-Fri., 0930-1230 Sat. Off Sauchiehall St. •Free.
Family-run gallery famous for its collection of old Glasgow photographs.

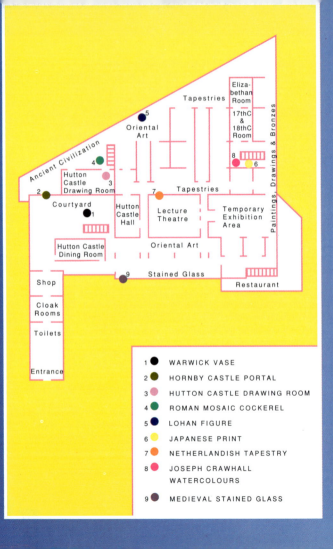

Tapestries

Eliza-
bethan
Room

17thC
&
18thC
Room

Paintings, Drawings & Bronzes

Oriental
Art

5

4

8

6

Ancient Civilization

Hutton
Castle
Drawing Room

3

Tapestries

2

7

Courtyard

1

Hutton
Castle
Hall

Lecture
Theatre

Temporary
Exhibition
Area

Oriental Art

Hutton Castle
Dining Room

9

Stained Glass

Shop

Restaurant

Cloak
Rooms

Toilets

Entrance

1 WARWICK VASE

2 HORNBY CASTLE PORTAL

3 HUTTON CASTLE DRAWING ROOM

4 ROMAN MOSAIC COCKEREL

5 LOHAN FIGURE

6 JAPANESE PRINT

7 NETHERLANDISH TAPESTRY

8 JOSEPH CRAWHALL
   WATERCOLOURS

9 MEDIEVAL STAINED GLASS

WARWICK VASE

Impressive 2ndC piece reconstructed from fragments found at the site of the Emperor Hadrian's villa at Tivoli near Rome in 1771. See **Burrell***.*

HORNBY CASTLE PORTAL

Early 16thC sandstone portal decorated with the heraldic emblems of William, Lord Conyers (1468-1524) and his feudal allies.

HUTTON CASTLE DRAWING ROOM

Largest of the three rooms from the Burrells' home in Berwick-on-Tweed; includes 16thC stained glass, Franco-Flemish tapestries, Persian rugs, oak furniture and medieval sculptures.

ROMAN MOSAIC COCKEREL

Exquisitely detailed fragment of a mosaic dating from the 1stC BC.

LOHAN FIGURE

Seated stoneware statue of a Lohan (a disciple of Buddha), dated 1484 (Ming Dynasty), serenely composed against the woodland backdrop.

JAPANESE PRINT Shoki The Demon Queller

Woodblock by Utagwa Kunisada (1786-1865) portraying the ferocious-looking Chinese Daoist god dispatching a struggling demon.

NETHERLANDISH TAPESTRY Hercules Initiating The Olympic Games

Allegorical depiction of the Burgundian court, including figures representing Duke Philip the Good and his son Charles the Bold, dated c. 1450-75.

JOSEPH CRAWHALL WATERCOLOURS

The only contemporary art collected by Burrell. Crawhall (1861-1913) was a member of the 'Glasgow Boys' who flourished in the city in the 1880s.

MEDIEVAL STAINED GLASS

13th-16thC English and Continental panels. They exhibit different styles and colours, and depict mostly religious subjects with some domestic scenes.

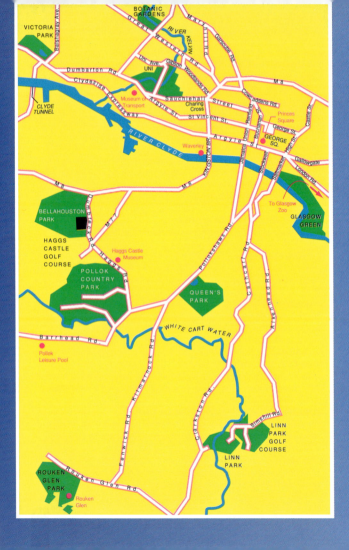

HAGGS CASTLE MUSEUM 100 St Andrew's Dr.
• 1000-1700 Mon.-Sat., 1400-1700 Sun. BR Glasgow Central to
Maxwell Park Station. Bus no. 59 from Union St. • Free.
Designed to help kids understand the past with special activities. See **A-Z**.

ROUKEN GLEN Rouken Glen Rd.
• Dawn-dusk daily. Bus nos. 38, 57 from Union Street. • Free.
• Butterfly Kingdom 1000-1730 daily (Mar.-Oct.). • £1.50, child £1.
*Beautiful parkland and the delightful Butterfly Kingdom full of exotic and
colourful species.*

GLASGOW ZOO Calderpark, Hamilton Rd, Uddingston.
• 1000-1700 (1800 summer). 10 km south east of the city on A74. Bus
nos. 44, 242 from Anderston Bus Station. • £2.50, child £1.40.
Wide variety of birds, mammals and reptiles.

MUSEUM OF TRANSPORT Kelvin Hall, Bunhouse Rd.
• 1000-1700 Mon.-Sat. 1400-1700 Sun. U Kelvinhall. • Free.
Vintage cars, old Glasgow trams, and much more. See **WALK 3**, **A-Z**.

POLLOK LEISURE POOL 27 Cowglen Rd.
• 1300-2115 Mon.-Tues. 1000-2115 Wed.-Fri., 1000-1615 Sat-Sun.
Bus Nos. 21, 21A, 23, 23A, 48 from Union St. • £1.10, child 60p.
The wave machine and water-slides are certain to keep the kids amused.

PRINCES SQUARE Buchanan St.
• 1000-2000 Mon.-Sat., 1130-1630 Sun. U St Enoch. • Free.
Daily entertainments and special events for children on Sun. afternoons.

WAVERLEY Anderston Quay.
Along the Broomielaw west of the Kingston Bridge. Tel: 221 8152.
• Weekend sailings from Glasgow to various destinations July-Aug.
• Children £2.95 all destinations.
*A pleasure cruise down the Firth of Clyde on the world's last sea-going pad-
dle steamer is ideal for children. There is often music and entertainment on
board, and a visit to the engine room is especially exciting.*

Glasgow

Newton
Mearns

A77

Kilmarnock

Dean
Castle

A77

Ayr

Belleisle
Gardens

Burns
Monument

Alloway
Dunure

Land O' Burns
Centre

A719

Electric
Brae

Culzean
Bay

A77

Culzean
Castle

Turnberry Golf
Course

Crossraguel Abbey

Kirkoswald

Souter Johnnie's Cottage

Turnberry

Royal Castle of Turnberry

Burns Country

From the city centre follow the signs for the A 77 south through Pollok and Newton Mearns.

37 km - Kilmarnock. Burns' poems were first published here on 31 July 1786 at John Wilson's Press (see **Burns**). At Kay Park (off the High Street) is the Burns Monument and Museum, and there is an annual Burns Festival in June/July. Other places of interest include the art gallery and museum in the Dick Institute and the Johnnie Walker whisky distillery founded in 1820. Dean Castle Country Park (entrance on the left 2 km after taking the Kilmarnock exit from the A 77) contains over 200 acres of parkland, rivers and gardens, and the 14thC castle houses Lord Howard's collection of European armour and the Van Raalte collection of musical instruments (1200-1700; £1.00, child free). Leave the town on the A 77 heading south.

65 km - Ayr. A popular seaside resort. The Auld Kirk (1655) is where Burns was baptized, the footbridge - the Auld Brig (1491) - features in Burns' poem *The Twa Brigs*, and the 'Tam O'Shanter Inn' is now a museum. After exploring the town (and the beach if the weather's fine) leave by the Dunure Road heading south.

70 km - Belleisle Gardens and Deer Park. Beautiful parklands, formal garden - and deer. 1.5 km south of Belleisle Gardens turn left for Alloway (then turn left at the junction ahead).

72 km - Alloway. The birthplace of the poet on 25 January 1759. Visit the Burns Cottage and Museum, and (500 m to the right of the junction) the Burns Monument (1823) and Garden, the Auld Brig O'Doon (which features in *Tam O'Shanter*) and the Land O'Burns Centre, a tourist centre and exhibition area concentrating on the poet's life and times. Return to the A 719 Dunure road and continue south following the coastline. 83 km turn right.

84 km - Dunure. A tiny village with a ruined castle that contains the Back Vault where the Earl of Cassillis reputedly roasted the Abbot of Crossraguel Abbey over a spit to force him to relinquish the abbey lands. Continue through Dunure (the route offers fine views of the Isle of Arran across the firth of Clyde to the east and south to Ailsa Craig), and turn right to return to the A 719.

90 km - The Electric Brae. Here you can experience an optical illusion which makes your car appear to be travelling downhill when actually

going up. 93 km turn right at the junction.

96 km - Culzean Castle and Country Park. The castle was designed by Robert Adam and built between 1777 and 1792 for the Earl of Cassillis, chief of the Kennedys, and has been beautifully restored by the National Trust for Scotland. It commands wonderful views over the lower Firth of Clyde from its clifftop position. Its other attractions include the magnificent oval staircase and round drawing room. The Eisenhower Presentation explores the former president's connection with the castle. The Country Park comprises 560 acres with walled garden, deer park, swan pond, aviary, guided walks, restaurant and tearooms. (1000 - 1800. Park £3.00 per car. Castle £2.10 extra, child £1.05). Continue on the A 719 south through Maidens.

104 km - Turnberry. Famous for its grand hotel and golf courses. There are also the ruins of the Royal Castle of Turnberry where Robert the Bruce, who later became King of Scots, spent his childhood. Just beyond the hotel turn left onto the A 77.

110 km - Kirkoswald. The location of Souter Johnnie's Cottage, the thatched dwelling of cobbler (Souter) John Davidson at the end of the 18thC, immortalized in *Tam O'Shanter*.

112 km - Crossraguel Abbey. The ruins (1244) of one of the few Cluniac settlements in Scotland. Continue north on the A 77.

185 km Glasgow.

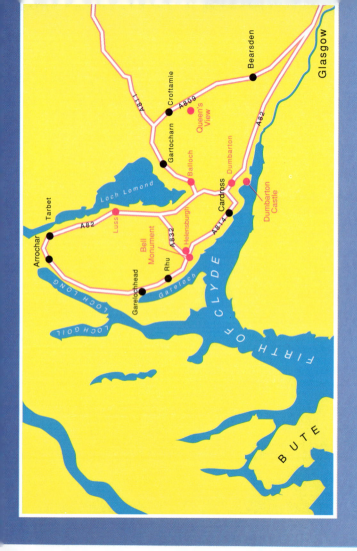

Loch Lomond

Follow the A 82 through Drumchapel and Duntocher along the north bank of the Clyde past the Erskine Bridge (1971). After 22 km turn left onto the A 814 for Dumbarton and Helensburgh.

24 km - **Dumbarton**. The ancient capital of the kingdom of Strathclyde. The castle (on Dumbarton Rock, which has a longer recorded history as a stronghold than anywhere else in Britain) commands magnificent views over the Firth of Clyde. In 1548 Mary Queen of Scots sailed from here to become the bride of Francis, King of France. Follow the High Street and cross the bridge over the River Leven and follow the A 814.

30 km - **Cardross**. Robert the Bruce died here in 1329.

37 km - **Helensburgh**. John Logie Baird, the inventor of radar and television, was born here in 1888. Along the front overlooking the Clyde estuary is an obelisk commemorating Henry Bell, the designer of the *Comet* (see **Broomielaw**). You should also visit Hill House designed by C. R. Mackintosh in 1902-4 (see **MACKINTOSH, A-Z**). Continue along the A 814 which runs parallel to the Gareloch past Rhu and Faslane, the home of Britain's nuclear submarine fleet.

55 km - **Garelochhead**. A small village and yachting harbour at the head of the loch. The A 814 now runs parallel to Loch Long on the left.

71 km - **Arrochar**. A small village overlooked by some fine peaks including Ben Arthur ('The Cobbler', 881 m), Ben Narnain (925 m) and Ben Ime (1011 m). Turn right past the village onto the A 83 to Tarbet, only 2 km away, then follow the A 82 down Loch Lomondside.

92 km - **Luss**. A pretty village visited by Coleridge, Wordsworth and Wordsworth's sister Dorothy in 1803. 5 km south is Rossdhu, a Georgian house and historic home of the chiefs of the Clan Colquhoun.

100 km - **Balloch**. On the River Leven. The paddle steamer *Maid of the Loch* leaves from the pier for daily trips. Other attractions include Cameron Bear Park; Cameron House and Balloch Castle Country Park - the castle is 19th century. Leave Balloch by the A 811 to Stirling; 119 km turn right onto the A 809 for Glasgow.

131 km - **Queen's View**. In 1879 Queen Victoria had her first view of Loch Lomond from here, and a short climb will reward you with same panorama over the Loch, its islands and the surrounding landscape. Follow the A 809 through Bearsden to the city centre.

156 km - **Glasgow**.

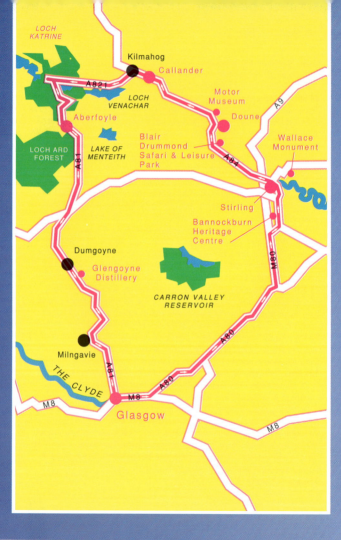

The Trossachs

Leave Glasgow on the M 8 then follow the A 80 and M 80 for Stirling.
42 km - leave the motorway at the signs for the tourist route to Stirling.
43 km - Bannockburn Heritage Centre. A tourist centre close to the memorial commemorating Robert the Bruce's victory over Edward II in 1314. Turn left out of the centre and follow the signs for Stirling.
50 km - Stirling. The historic castle perches on a volcanic plug of rock 76 m above the town (0930-1715 Mon.-Sat., 1030-1645 Sun. £1.50, child 75p, under 5s free). It dates back to the Middle Ages and was the royal residence of the Stuart kings. Its attractions include the Chapel Royal (where Mary Queen of Scots was crowned), the Great Hall and the Regimental Museum of the Argyll and Sutherland Highlanders. There are splendid views from Castle Rock west to Ben Lomond and the Trossachs, and the Ochil Hills to the east. There is also a clear view of the Wallace Monument towering above the surrounding woods to the east which commemorates Sir William Wallace, the Scottish guerilla hero of the 13thC Wars of Independence against the English (reached by the A 9 from Stirling to Causewayhead then follow the signs on the A 91. Open from 1000 Feb.-Oct. £1.20, child 60p). Leave Stirling by the A 84 (follow the signs for Doune and Callander). Beyond the town on the right is Blair Drummond Safari and Leisure Park, which has a wild animal reserve (1000-1630 Mar.-Oct. £3.50, child 2.50).
68 km - Doune. Visit the ruins of the 14thC castle, one of the best preserved medieval castles in Scotland (0930-1900 Mon.-Sat., 1400-1900 Sun. Apr.-Sept. 60p, child 30p). Just beyond Doune is the Motor Museum (1000-1730, June-Aug., 1000-1700 Sept.-May. £1.90, child under 16 90p, under 5s free) which contains a superb collection of 40 classic cars, including the second-oldest Rolls Royce in the world.
85 km - Callander. The heart of the Trossachs. Carry on through the town to Kilmahog, then turn left onto the A 821 to Aberfoyle passing Loch Venachar on the left. 100 km - carry on through the junction.
101 km - Loch Katrine. A reservoir which supplies Glasgow's water. There are regular sailings from the pier. Back at the junction turn right.
109 km - Aberfoyle. A pretty tourist centre. Return to Glasgow on A 81.
131 km - Glengoyne Distillery. Produces a fine malt whisky, visitors are welcome (guided tours £1.50, child 50p).
160 km - Glasgow.

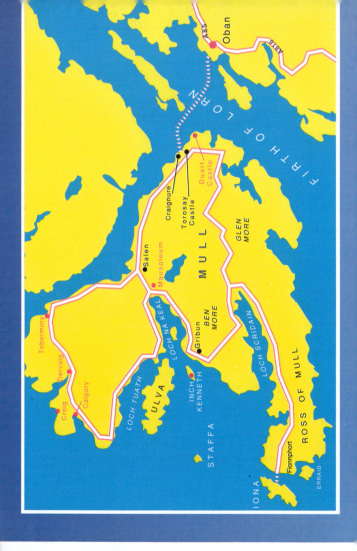

EXCURSION 4

Isle of Mull

2 - 3 days. Overnight stay on Mull or Iona.

Oban is 154 km by car from Glasgow, following a gloriously scenic route along the A 82 heading north, past Loch Lomond (see **EXCURSION 2**), and then west on the A 85 from Crianlarich.

A popular holiday resort, Oban is situated on a sheltered bay surrounded by wooded hills. Overlooking the bay is McCaig's Tower, a late 19thC memorial to a local banker, which encloses a landscaped garden. As well as admiring the scenery, you can visit the Caithness Glass factory (south of the town centre) and watch the manufacture of their famous products (0900-1700 Mon.-Fri., shop also 0900-1300 Sat. during May and Sept.; tour free). 'A World in Miniature' on the North Pier is a fascinating display of models, miniature furniture and dioramas by master craftsmen (1000-1800 Mon.-Sat., 1400-1800 Sun. 80p, child 50p). Oban is also called the 'Gateway to the Isles' and ferries depart regularly to the Outer and Inner Hebrides (tel: (0631) 62285 for details of all services - it's best to book in advance).

Mull is the third-largest of the Hebridean Islands, and offers visitors a variety of attractions, including rugged scenery, castles and museums. Most of the roads are single-lane and frequently blocked by sheep, so drive carefully. The ferry service runs from Oban to Craignure, and the crossing takes about 45 minutes. A miniature railway runs from the pier for 3 km to Torosay Castle (1030-1730 May-Sept.). Just south of Craignure is Duart Castle (1030-1800 May-Sept.), the medieval base of the Clan Maclean, which guards the approach to Mull (the ferry passes close by before Craignure). The main road continues west through the countryside of Glen More, then divides at the head of Loch Scridain for the west of Mull or Fionnphort on the Ross of Mull. On the south-western tip of the Ross is the islet of Erraid which was once the home of the author Robert Louis Stevenson. From Fionnphort it is only a ten-minute crossing to Iona, a beautiful and historic island which is definitely worth visiting. St Columba arrived here from Ireland in 563 and established the first church in Scotland, bringing Christianity to the Highlands and Islands. Visit the cathedral (the burial-place of many early Scottish kings) and abbey buildings, and experience the unique tranquility of this sacred spot. The island has several hotels, making possible an overnight stay before returning to explore the rest of Mull.

The western side of Mull, bitten into by the great sea lochs, contains some of the most beautiful coastal scenery in Scotland and is superb walking country. The route passes Ben More (a relatively easy climb) which offers breathtaking views from its summit. Inch Kenneth, seen from the clifftops beyond Gribun, is the site of a house which belonged to the Mitford family. Dr Johnson stayed here during his famous tour of the Highlands and Islands. At the head of Loch Na Keal (look out for the signpost on the right-hand side of the road) is the mausoleum of Lachlan MacQuarrie, the 'Father of Australia', a victim of the Highland Clearances who became the first Governor of New South Wales. Follow the road inland to Salen, then head north for Tobermory, the island's capital, and one of the safest and most beautiful anchorages in the Hebrides. At the bottom of the harbour lies the wreck of a Spanish galleon, one of the ships of the Armada which anchored here after the Spanish defeat in 1588. The cause of the wreck is unclear; one version states it was blown up by Maclean of Duart, another that it was the result of witchcraft. The wreck is supposed to contain valuable treasure, although various attempts to salvage it have failed.

If you wish, instead of heading across to Salen, you can reach Tobermory via Calgary (after which the Canadian city is named) along the narrow and twisting route which skirts the shores of Loch Tuath. Calgary has the best beach on the island, a deep bay with fine white sands framed by wooded slopes. Croig, to the north, commands the best sea-view on Mull, overlooking the islands of Rhum, Muck, Eigg, Canna and the Cuillin Hills on Skye. Directly ahead you can also see Ardnamurchan Point, the most westerly point of the British mainland. Dervaig, at the head of Loch a' Chuinn, is one of the prettiest villages on the island. The Old Byre Heritage Centre has a craftshop and muse-um whose exhibits describe crofting life and the cruel drama of the Highland Clearances (1020-1830 Mar.-Oct.; £1, children under 12 50p). From Dervaig the road descends across the Mishnish headland to Tobermory. Return to Craignure along the A 849.

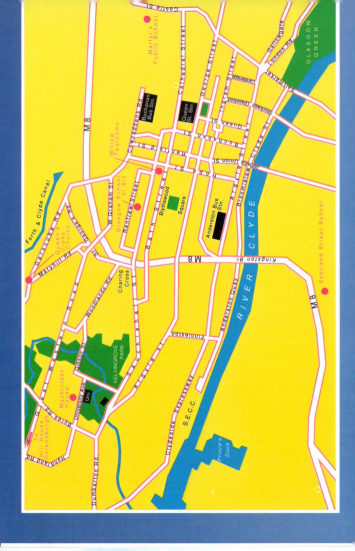

GLASGOW SCHOOL OF ART 167 Renfrew St.
● Guided tours by appointment only, tel: 332 9797 (ext 216).
U Cowcaddens.
Mackintosh's most celebrated building, completed in 1907-8 and now regarded as a landmark in modern architecture. See **Mackintosh**, WALK 2.

HILL HOUSE Upper Colquhoun St. Helensburgh.
● 1300-1630. BR from Queen Street Station. ● £1.50, child 90p.
Built for the publisher Walter W. Blackie between 1902-4, the finest example of Mackintosh's domestic designs. See EXCURSION 2.

MACKINTOSH HOUSE Glasgow University, 82 Hillhead St.
● 0930-1230, 1330-1700 Mon.-Fri. 0930-1300 Sat. In the Hunterian Art Gallery. U Hillhead. ● 50p. (Free on weekday mornings).
A reconstruction on three floors of the architect's former Glasgow home.

MARTYR'S PUBLIC SCHOOL Parson St.
● 0930-1700. Tours by appointment, tel: 552 2104. 10 minutes' walk north east of George Square. ● Free.
Mackintosh's first building (1895) but the style is unmistakable.

QUEEN'S CROSS CHURCH 780 Garscube Rd.
● 1200-1700 Tues., Thurs., Fri. 1430-1700 Sun. At the junction of Maryhill Rd and Garscube Rd. Bus nos. 13, 18, 29, 61, 61A. ● Free.
Dating from 1897, this important building is now home of the Charles Rennie Mackintosh Society.

SCOTLAND STREET SCHOOL 225 Scotland St.
● Tours by appointment only, tel: 429 1202. U Shields Road.
This red sandstone building's most striking features are the external glass bays enclosing the staircases. It now houses the Museum of Education.

WILLOW TEAROOMS 217 Sauchiehall St.
● 0930-1630 Mon.-Sat. U Cowcaddens. ● Free.
Designed for restauranteur Miss Kate Cranston in 1903, the frontage and interior have been restored to the original design. See WALK 2.

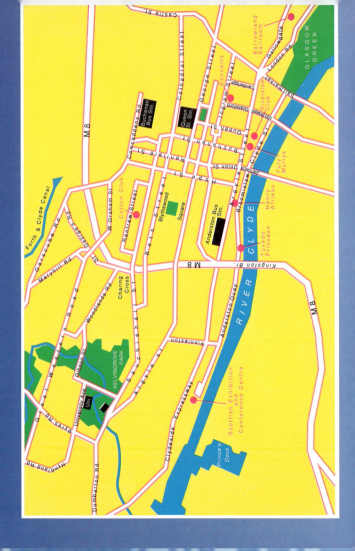

BENNETTS 90 Glassford St.
• 2300-0300 Tues., Thurs. 2300-0330 Fri.-Sun. Near George Sq. • £3.
Popular Gay nightspot although all are welcome.

COTTON CLUB 5 Scott St.
• 2300-0330 Wed.-Sun. Off Sauchiehall St. behind Cannon Cinema.
• £3 Wed., Fri.; £5 Sat.; £2.50 before midnight Sun.
Small upmarket nightclub favoured by the fashionable set.

HENRY AFRIKAS 15 York St.
• 2230-0330 Wed.,Thurs., 2300-0400 Fri., 2230-0330 Sat.
U St Enoch. • £4 Sat. (£2-£3 other nights).
One of the city's most popular and successful clubs.

FURY MURRYS 96 Maxwell St.
• 2230-0300 Wed., Thurs., Sun.; 2230-0330 Fri., Sat.
U St Enoch. • £3-£4.
One of Glasgow's best nightclubs; live music Thursday nights.

RIVERSIDE CLUB Fox St.
• 2200-0200 Fri.-Sat. U St Enoch. • £3.
Lively Ceildh every Friday and Saturday night for those with energy to enjoy the furious pace of traditional Scottish dancing and music.

TUXEDO PRINCESS Broomielaw.
• 1200-0300. Moored near the Kingston Bridge.
• £3 after 2100 Mon.-Thurs.; £5 after 2100 Fri., Sat.; £2 Sun.
Ex car-ferry now a glittering nightspot: nine bars, two discos and restaurant.

BARROWLAND BALLROOM 244 Gallowgate.
Ten minutes' walk from Glasgow Cross. Tickets from Virgin Records.
Small rock venue featuring the best contemporary rock and pop bands.

SCOTTISH EXHIBITION AND CONFERENCE CENTRE
Finnieston St. Off the Clydeside Expressway. Tel: 204 2161.
Massive venue for concerts by world megastars.

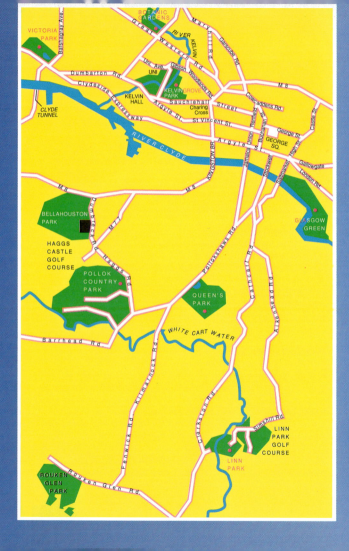

PARKS

BOTANIC GARDENS Gt Western Rd.
• Dawn-dusk daily. Kibble Palace 1000-1645 (winter 1615). Main Glasshouse 1300-1645 (winter 1615) Mon.-Sat.; 1200-1645 Sun. U Hillhead. •Free.
Contains the famous Kibble Palace. See **A-Z**.

GLASGOW GREEN Greendyke St.
• Dawn-dusk daily. On north bank of the Clyde off Saltmarket. •Free.
Has a long and varied history at the centre of Glasgow life. See **WALK 1**, **A-Z**.

KELVINGROVE PARK Argyle St.
• Dawn-dusk daily. U Kelvinhall. •Free.
85 acres beside the University and Art Gallery. See **WALK 3**, **A-Z**.

LINN PARK Clarkston Rd.
• Dawn-dusk daily. 6 km south of the city. Bus nos. 5A, 31, 34 from St Enoch Sq. •Free.
200 acres of woodland, a ruined 14th-century castle, riverside walks, nature trails, a children's zoo, ponies and Highland Cattle.

POLLOK COUNTRY PARK 2060 Pollokshaws Rd.
• Dawn-dusk daily. Bus Nos. 9, 21, 45, 48, 57, 59 from Union St.
• Free.
Huge area of parkland and gardens with nature trails, Ranger Centre, rose garden, Highland Cattle. Site of the Burrell Collection and Pollok House.

QUEEN'S PARK Victoria Rd.
• Dawn-dusk daily. Bus no. 44 from Union St. •Free.
Named after Mary Queen of Scots; boating pond, woodlands, picnic areas and formal gardens.

VICTORIA PARK Victoria Park Drive North.
• Dawn-dusk daily. Fossil Grove 0800-1600 Mon.-Fri.; Sat., Sun. afternoon only. Bus no. 93 from St Enoch Sq. •Free.
Formal gardens and boating pond. Also site of the intriguing Fossil Grove containing prehistoric tree stumps which date back 330 million years.

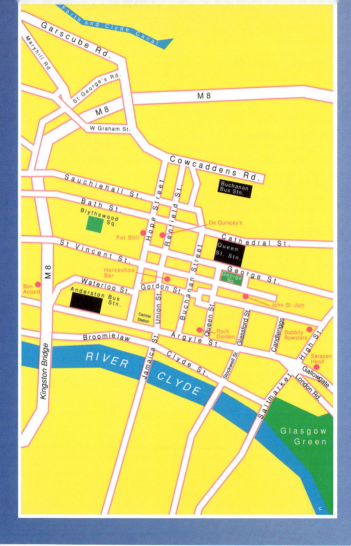

BABBITY BOWSTERS 15-18 Blackfriars St.
Off the High Street five minutes' walk from Glasgow Cross.
A stylish café/bar with outdoor patio, great food and regular live folk music, drama and poetry readings.

BON-ACCORD 153 North St.
Beside the Mitchell Library.
Superb Real Ales with outlandish and amusing names like 'Ringwood Old Thumper' and 'Marston's Pedigree'. Excellent wines for a Glasgow bar.

DE QUINCEY'S 71 Renfield St.
Attractive wine bar with colonial-style decor and atmosphere. Good range of wines and buffet meals.

THE HORSESHOE BAR 17 Drury St.
Across from Central Station off Renfield St.
One of the city's most famous pubs. Has a magnificent horseshoe-shaped bar and original Victorian decor.

JOHN STREET JAM 18 John St.
Near George Square.
A large bar and diner with New Orleans jazz motif.

POT STILL 154 Hope St.
Handy if you want to sample a traditional Malt whisky - it has an impressive selection of over 280 different brands !

ROCK GARDEN 73 Queen St.
Off Argyle St. towards George Square.
Lively bar packed with pop memorabilia.

SARACEN HEAD Gallowgate.
East of Glasgow Cross.
A living symbol of the old Glasgow which is rapidly being overwhelmed by the new, clean, sober image. The building dates from 1755 and some of the regulars (mostly men) look as though they've been drinking there ever since.

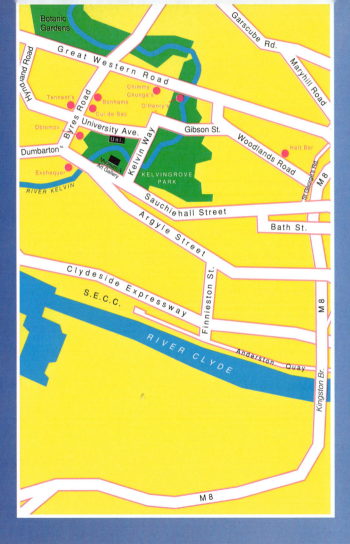

West End

BONHAMS 194 Byres Rd.
U Hillhead.
Popular wine bar decorated with a miscellany of weird objects.

CHIMMY CHUNGA'S 499 Gt Western Rd.
U Kelvinbridge.
Mexican theme pub.

CUL DE SAC 46 Ashton Lane.
U Hillhead.
Quite fashionable but the drinks are pricier than some of the more traditional pubs in nearby Byres Road.

EXCHEQUER 59 Dumbarton Rd.
U Kelvinhall.
Spacious pub with gallery area upstairs. The building has an 'art nouveau' facade and there is a beer garden at the back.

HALT BAR 160 Woodlands Rd.
U St George's Cross.
Popular West End pub with a traditional horseshoe bar and small lounge which regularly hosts folk and jazz evenings.

OBLOMOV 116 Byres Rd.
U Hillhead.
Dutch theme pub. The bar/bistro section serves excellent food.

O'HENRY'S CAFÉ/BAR 445 Gt Western Rd.
U Kelvinbridge.
Built into the archway of the bridge. In summer you can enjoy a drink sitting outside overlooking the River Kelvin.

TENNENT'S Byres Rd.
U Hillhead.
Traditional, unpretentious pub frequented by the serious drinking fraternity of all age groups.

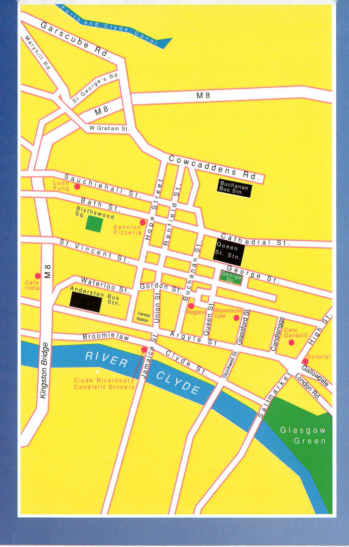

City Centre

COLONIAL 25 High St.
• 1200-1430,1800-2230 Mon.-Sat. (closed Mon. evening). At the southern end of High St. • Expensive. Tel: 552 1923.
Modern French and Scottish cuisine. Best to book at weekends.

ROGANO 11 Exchange Pl.
• 1200-1430, 1900-2230 Mon.-Sat. ∪ St Enoch. • Expensive. Tel: 248 4055.
Exotic art deco interior and unique atmosphere. Specializes in succulent seafood dishes.

CAFÉ INDIA 171 North St., Charing Cross.
• 1200-1430, 1700-2400 Mon.-Thurs., 1200-2400 Fri., Sat, 1700-2400 Sun. Beside the Mitchell Library. • Moderate.
Excellent curries and a large selection of wines and beers.

CLYDE RIVERBOAT CANDLELIT DINNERS 31 Broomielaw.
• 1930-2230 Thurs., Fri., Sat. At the end of Jamaica St. under the Railway Bridge. Tel: 221 8702. • Moderate.
Something different. Heated and enclosed. Booking essential.

LOON FUNG 417 Sauchiehall St.
• 1200-2330 daily. • Moderate-Expensive.
The best Cantonese food in the city centre.

CAFÉ GANDOLFI 64 Albion St.
• 0930-2330 Mon.-Sat. Behind the City Halls. • Inexpensive-Moderate.
Delightful and stylish bar/bistro serving appetizing French and Scottish food.

SANNINO PIZZERIA 61 Bath St.
• 1200-2400 Mon.-Sat. • Inexpensive-Moderate.
Superb pizzas and pasta dishes at reasonable prices for the city centre.

WAREHOUSE CAFÉ Top Floor, 61 Glassford St.
• 1000-1800 Mon.-Sat. • Inexpensive-Moderate.
Third-floor café overlooking the Merchant City, with a wide-ranging menu.

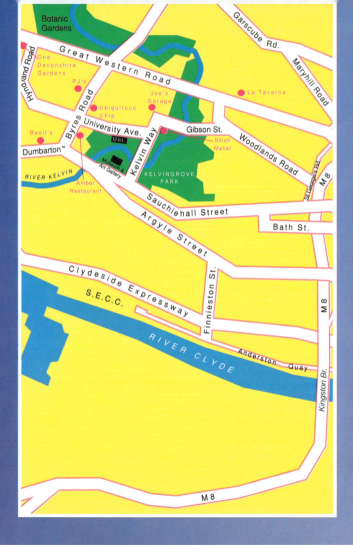

RESTAURANTS

ONE DEVONSHIRE GARDENS 1 Devonshire Gardens.
• 1230-1400, 1900-2200 Mon.-Sat. (closed Sat. lunchtime). Off Hyndland Rd at junction with Gt Western Rd. • Expensive.
Up-market hotel and restaurant in a mid-Victorian terraced building.

UBIQUITOUS CHIP 2 Ashton Lane.
• 1200-1430, 1730-2300 Mon.-Sat. U Hillhead. • Expensive.
Fashionable Scottish cuisine in a leafy courtyard setting. Upstairs bar.

AMBER 130 Byres Rd.
• 1700-2330 Mon.-Wed., 1200-1415, 1700-2400 Thurs., Fri., 1200-2400 Sat., 1700-2330 Sun. U Hillhead. • Moderate.
Superb Cantonese food. The West End's answer to the Loon Fung.

LA TAVERNA 7A Lansdowne Crescent.
• 1200-1400, 1800-2300 Mon.-Fri., 1800-2300 Sat.,1830-2300 Sun. U Kelvinbridge. • Moderate.
One of the best Italian restaurants in the West End.

SHISH MAHAL 45 Gibson St.
• 1145-2330. U Kelvinbridge. • Moderate.
Popular, high-quality Indian restaurant in the student area.

BASIL'S VEGETARIAN CAFÉ 184 Dumbarton Rd.
• 1200-2130 Sun., Mon., Wed., 1830-2130 Tues., 1200-2300 Thurs.-Sat U Kelvinhall. • Inexpensive-Moderate.
Small licensed café specializing in vegetarian and vegan dishes.

JOE'S GARAGE 52 Bank St.
• 1200-0030. U Kelvinbridge. • Inexpensive
Genuinely delicious burgers.

P. J.'S Ruthven Lane.
• 1200-1430, 1700-2400 Mon.-Fri., 1200-2400 Sat, Sun. U Hillhead. • Inexpensive.
Good-quality, if rather unconventional, pasta dishes.

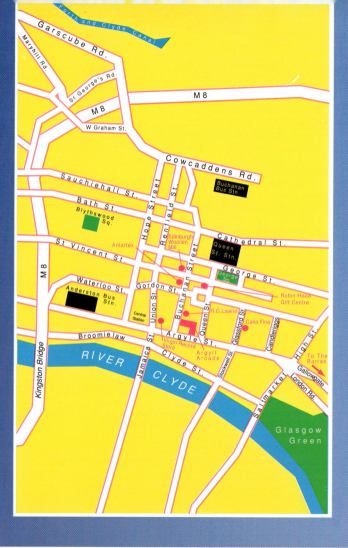

R. G. LAWRIE LTD 110 Buchanan St.
•0900-1730 Mon.-Sat. U Buchanan St.
Top-quality tartans, tweeds, woollens, kilts and accessories, jewellery and glassware.

EDINBURGH WOOLLEN MILL 22 Nelson Mandela Place.
•0900-1730 Mon.-Sat. U Buchanan Street.
Stocks a good range of quality knitwear at reasonable prices.

ANTARTEX 127 Buchanan St.
•0900-1730 Mon.-Sat. U Buchanan St.
Good-value sheepskin coats, jackets, gloves and other items to help combat the Scottish climate.

ARGYLL ARCADE Buchanan St.
•0900-1730. U St Enoch.
Large concentration of jewellery shops under one roof. See **A-Z**.

ROBIN HOOD GIFT HOUSE 11 St Vincent Place.
•0900-1730 Mon.-Sat. U Buchanan St.
Large selection of souvenirs including crystal, jewellery, whisky items and tartan memorabilia.

CASA FINA 2 Wilson Court, Wilson Street.
•0930-1730 Mon.-Fri., 0930-1800 Sat.
Small shop in the Merchant City stocking an unusual range of home furnishings and gifts.

VIRGIN RECORDS 28 Union St.
•0900-1800 Mon.-Sat. U St Enoch.
The largest record store in Glasgow.

THE BARRAS 244 Gallowgate.
East of Glasgow Cross between the Gallowgate and London Rd.
•0900-1700 Sat., Sun.
Glasgow's famous street market. See **A-Z**.

Forth and Clyde Canal

Garscube Rd.

Maryhill Rd.

St George's Rd.

M 8

M 8

W Graham St.

Cowcaddens Rd.

Sauchiehall St.

Buchanan
Bus Stn.

Cooper
Hay
Rare
Books

Bath St.

Tim
Wright
Antiques

Hope Street

Renfield St.

Blythswood
Sq.

Cathedral St.

Queen
St. Stn.

St Vincent St.

Buchanan St.

George St.

M 8

George
Sq.

Waterloo St.

Gordon St.

Anderston Bus
Stn.

Union St.

Central
Station

Broomielaw

Jamaica St.

Argyle St.

Queen St.

Princes
Square

Glassford St.

Miki

Inhouse

Candleriggs

Ichi
Ni San

High St.

Lewis's

Clyde St.

Stockwell St.

Boutique
Homme

Gallowgate

London Rd.

Kingston Bridge

RIVER

CLYDE

St Enoch
Centre

Saltmarket

Glasgow
Green

PRINCES SQUARE Buchanan Street.
• 1000-1900 Mon.-Sat., 1130-1630 Sun. Restaurants open till 2400.
U Buchanan Street.
Stylish shopping mall with a variety of unusual, expensive boutiques.

ST ENOCH CENTRE
• 0800-1900. U St Enoch.
Massive glass-covered shopping centre.

LEWIS'S Argyle St.
• 0900-1730 Mon.-Sat. U St Enoch.
Glasgow's largest department store, handy for practically any item.

BOUTIQUE HOMME 2 Glassford Court, Glassford St.
• 0930-1800 Mon.-Sat. (1900 Thurs.).
Stylish menswear from top designers such as Valentino and Ungaro.

ICHI NI SAN 123 Candleriggs.
• 1000-1900 Mon.-Sat., 1130-1630 Sun. In the Merchant City.
Designer clothes and accessories for both men and women.

MIKI 7 Garth St.
• 1000-1730 Mon.-Sat. In the Merchant City.
Specializes in clothes for babies and children.

INHOUSE 24-26 Wilson St.
• 1000-1800 Mon.-Sat. (1900 Thurs.). In the Merchant City.
Furniture, lighting and other items in exciting contemporary designs.

TIM WRIGHT ANTIQUES 147 Bath St.
• 0930-1700 Mon.-Sat. On corner of West Campbell St.
Beautiful furniture, ceramics, glass and metalware.

COOPER HAY RARE BOOKS 203 Bath St.
• 1000-1700 Mon.-Fri., 1000-1300 Sat.
Glasgow's leading antiquarian book and print dealer.

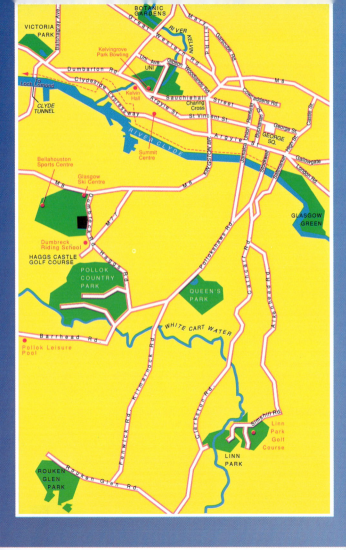

BOWLING Kelvingrove Park, Argyle St.
•0900-1700 daily. U Kelvinhall. •65p an hour.
Pleasant well-kept greens beside the Museum and Art Gallery. There are also tennis courts opposite and a putting green nearby.

CYCLING Loch Lomond Cycle Route.
A 34 km cycle route from the centre of Glasgow to Loch Lomond, following disused railway tracks and waterside paths and avoiding roads as much as possible. Ideal for families and novices as well as enthusiasts.
See **Bicycle Hire**, **Tourist Information**.

GOLF Linn Park, Simshill Rd.
•Open from 0800. 6 km south of city off B766. •£2.10 Mon.-Fri., £2.70 Sat., Sun.
18-hole course which places no restrictions on visitors.

HORSE RIDING Dumbreck Riding School, 82 Dumbreck Rd.
•1000-1500 Mon.-Fri., 0900-1700 Sat, Sun. In Pollok Country Park. Bus no. 59 from Union St. •£5 per hour. Tel: 427 0660.
Riding instruction and accompanied rides around Pollok estate. Book in advance.

ICE SKATING The Summit Centre, Minerva Way, Finnieston.
•0930-1200, 1400-1630, 1900-2200 Sat. 1330-1600, 1900-2200 Sun. Off Clydeside Expressway. •Children under 12 £1, over 12 £1.50, evenings £2. Tel: 204 2215.
Skate hire and tuition available; the evening sessions are actually ice discos.

SKIING Glasgow Ski Centre, Bellahouston Park, 16 Dumbreck Rd.
U Cessnock. •£10 including ski and boot hire. Tel: 427 4991.
A dry slope which caters for beginners and the more advanced.

SWIMMING Pollok Leisure Pool, 27 Cowglen Rd.
•1300-2115 Mon.-Tues., 1000-2115 Wed.-Fri., 1000-1615 Sat.-Sun.
•£1.10, child 60p. Tel: 881 3313.
Good facilities for serious swimmers as well as fun for the whole family.

BELLAHOUSTON SPORTS CENTRE, Bellahouston Dr.
•0920-2245. Corner of Bellahouston Park off Paisley Rd West.
U Cessnock. Bus nos. 9, 52, 54 from city centre. Tel: 427 5454.
Facilities for a comprehensive range of sports including aerobics, badminton, carpet bowls, fencing, karate, athletics, squash and many more.

KELVIN HALL, Argyle St.
•0900-2230 daily. U Kelvinhall. Tel: 357 2525.
Venue for international athletics and other sporting events, but also provides indoor courts for badminton, football, squash; a running track and conditioning gym. See **WALK 3**.

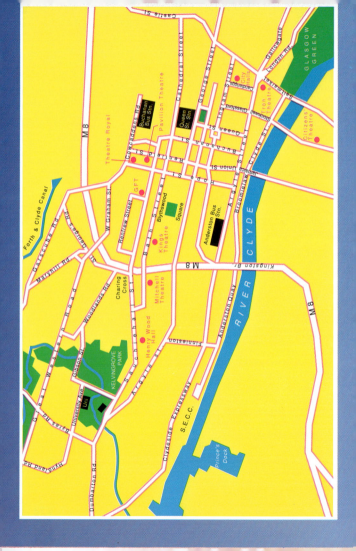

CITIZENS' THEATRE 119 Gorbals St.
•Sept.-March. •All seats £3. U Bridge St.
Home of the world-famous company with a reputation for staging exciting, innovative and often controversial drama productions.

CITY HALLS Candleriggs.
South east of George Sq.
Small hall used for musical concerts ranging from classical to folk and rock.

GLASGOW FILM THEATRE 12 Rose St.
Off Sauchiehall St. •£2.70, child £1.50.
Presents a stimulating programme of British and Continental films.

HENRY WOOD HALL 73 Claremont St.
Off Sauchiehall St. past Charing Cross. Bus no. 57 from Union Street.
Home of the Scottish National Orchestra.

KING'S THEATRE Bath St.
At the end of Bath St. near Charing Cross.
Popular comedy drama, musicals and pantomimes.

MITCHELL THEATRE Granville St.
In the extension to the Mitchell Library.
Presents local drama and touring productions.

PAVILION THEATRE 121 Renfield St.
Near the junction with Sauchiehall St.
Popular variety acts, music, hypnotists, comedy and drama.

THEATRE ROYAL 282 Hope St.
U Cowcaddens.
The home of the Scottish Opera, also prestigious ballet and drama.

TRON THEATRE 38 Parnie St.
Near Glasgow Cross.
New drama, touring productions, fringe comedy and experimental material.

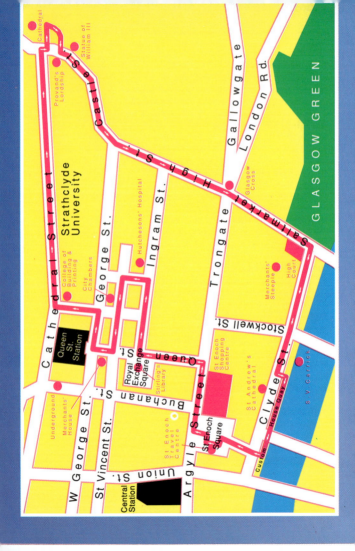

East End

2 hours 30 min. Start in George Square (see **A-Z**). On the east side are the City Chambers (see **A-Z**), on the west side is the Merchants' House, home of the Glasgow Chamber of Commerce founded in 1783. Leave by North Frederick St. and walk up the hill. Turn right at the top of the hill into Cathedral St. On the right as you walk along are the University of Strathclyde campus buildings (see **A-Z**). Carry on through the T-junction and turn right into Castle St. Just down on the right is Provand's Lordship (1471), the oldest surviving house in Glasgow (see **A-Z**). Cross over into the Cathedral Precinct to visit the Cathedral, one of the most historic buildings in the city (see **A-Z**). As you leave the Cathedral, turn left into Castle St. and walk down the hill into the High St. On the left is an equestrian statue (1735) of William III, which was originally in the Trongate. At the foot of the High St. is Glasgow Cross (see **A-Z**), the heart of the 17thC city. The Tolbooth Steeple (see **A-Z**) dates from 1626. The Mercat (market) Cross nearby marks the site of a market held in the city in medieval times. Continue down into the Saltmarket. On the left is Glasgow Green (see **A-Z**). On the right is the High Court (1807-14) by William Stark; only the Greek portico survives from the original design. Turn right into Clyde St. Walk along past the Briggait Centre, from which rises the 16thC Merchants' Steeple. On the river is the SV *Carrick*, an old sailing vessel now the HQ of the Royal Naval Volunteer Reserve. On the right is St Andrew's Cathedral (1816) the first Gothic Revival church in Glasgow, and beside it the modern glass frontage of the offices of the Archdiocese of Glasgow. Opposite the cathedral walk along Custom House Quay past the suspension bridge. Rejoin the road and turn right into Dixon St. which leads into St Enoch Square. On the right is the commanding edifice of the glass-roofed shopping complex (see **SHOPPING 2**). Walk past the old underground station ticket office (1896), now the Travel Centre. Turn right into Argyle St., the main shopping area in the city. Cross the road and walk past the entrance to the Argyll Arcade (see **SHOPPING 1**, **A-Z**) and turn left into Queen St. Ahead and on the left is Royal Exchange Square and Stirling's Library (see **A-Z**) with the statue of Wellington in front. Turn right into Ingram St. Ahead is Hutchesons' Hospital (see **A-Z**). Turn left up John St. On the left on the corner of Cochrane St. is the Italian Centre and ahead are the City Chambers. Turn left back to George Square.

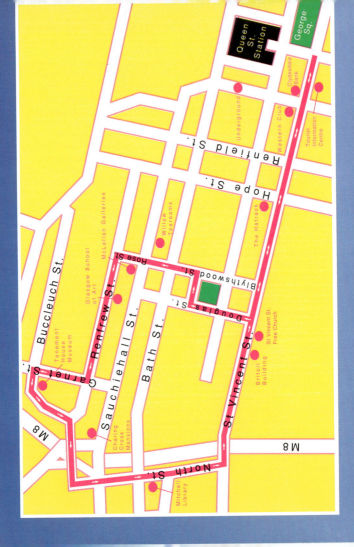

2 hours 30 min. Start in St Vincent Place beside the Tourist Information Office. Opposite is the Clydesdale Bank (1870-3) by John Burnet, one of the finest examples of Palladian architecture in Europe. Walk along to the junction with Buchanan St. On the right hand corner is the former Western Club (1840-41) by David Hamilton, perhaps his most notable building. Follow St Vincent St. up the hill. Just beyond the junction with Hope St. on the right, at Nos. 142-44, is the eight-storey building by James Salmon Jnr (1899) known as the 'Hatrack' because of its unusually tall and slim design. Beside it is the modern glass frontage of the Scottish Amicable Building (1977). Continue up St Vincent St., turn right into Douglas St. and enter Blythswood Square (see **A-Z**). Leave the Square by Blythswood St. which leads onto Sauchiehall St. pedestrian precinct, a favourite area for pavement artists. Turn right and a few yards down are the Willow Tearooms (see **MACKINTOSH**). Opposite the tearooms to the left enter Rose St. On the left are the McLellan Galleries (see **A-Z**) and on the right is the Glasgow Film Theatre (see **THEATRE**). Turn left into Renfrew St. A short walk up the hill is the Glasgow School Of Art (see **MACKINTOSH**). Continue along Renfrew St. then turn right into Garnet St., just over the hill turn left into Buccleuch St., ahead on the corner is the Tenement House Museum (see **ART & CULTURE**, **A-Z**).

Turn the corner and take the right fork of the path ahead which slopes down the hill to rejoin Renfrew St. Cross the bridge over the M8 motorway, turn left and walk down to Charing Cross past the drinking fountain. Cross at the lights and stop to look back across the busy junction to Charing Cross Mansions (1891) by the Glasgow architect J. J. Burnet, an elaborately decorated tenement block with a Baroque clock and carved figures. Follow North St., on the right is the Mitchell Library (see **A-Z**). Carry on beside the M 8 motorway past the Café India (see **RESTAURANTS 2**) and Bon-Accord (see **PUBS**) until the junction with St Vincent St. Turn left and walk along St Vincent St. up the hill. On the right is the Britoil Building (which boasts a rooftop landscaped garden) and beside it St Vincent St. Free Church (1858) by Alexander 'Greek' Thomson, the city's most original architect after Mackintosh; note the tower which combines classical and Italianate design. Follow St Vincent St. back over the hill to St Vincent Place.

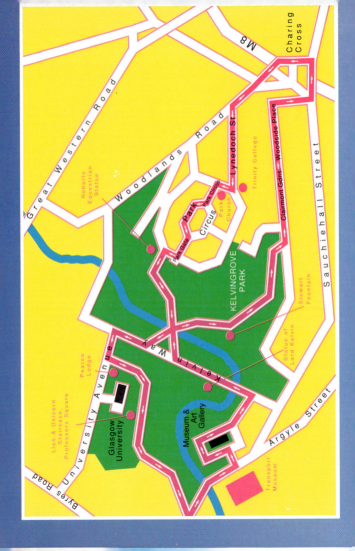

West End

2 hours 30 min.

Start at Charing Cross at the end of Sauchiehall St. Walk round to the right and cross the busy junction onto Woodlands Rd. Turn left into Lynedoch St. and walk up the hill. The tower on the left belongs to Trinity College (formerly Free Church College, and now upmarket residences) designed by Charles Wilson in 1854. Continue into Park Circus Place. On the corner is the tower of Park Church (1858) now converted into modern offices. Ahead is Park Circus (1850s), again by Charles Wilson and a masterpiece of Victorian urban design. Follow the road round the Circus and leave by Park Gate. Straight ahead is the entrance to Kelvingrove Park (see PARKS). Just inside the entrance to the park is the memorial to Earl Roberts of Kandahar (1834-1914), a famous soldier. From here there is a pleasant view over the Glasgow University buildings, with the University library to the right and Kelvingrove Art Gallery and Museum to the left, and the now silent shipyards beyond. Take the path to the left, walk on past the junction of paths, following the route straight on down the hill towards the bridge over the River Kelvin. At the foot of the hill is a memorial to the soldiers of the Highland Light Infantry who fell during the Boer War 1899-1902. Cross the bridge - ahead is a statue of Thomas Carlyle (1795-1881) - turn right and follow the path up to Kelvin Way. Keep right and then turn left onto University Avenue. On the left is the Pearce Lodge gatehouse, constructed from fragments of the Old College (1656) which was demolished when the University moved to Gilmorehill in the 1870s. Turn left through the gatehouse and walk up the road which winds uphill past the James Watt Building on the right to the front of the main University Buildings (see **A-Z**) designed by Sir George Gilbert Scott (1866-70). There is a beautiful view from the the base of the flagpole over the Art Gallery & Museum below. You can walk through the arches into the calm and cool of the magnificent Gothic central range between the Quadrangles, or visit the Hunterian Museum (see ART & CULTURE). Along on the right past the front of the building is the entrance to Professors' Square. Just inside the gate is the Lion and Unicorn Staircase (1691), another fragment from the Old College building. Leave the Square and return to the front of the building, turn right and follow the path down the hill to the left where it joins Argyle St.

Turn left and cross Partick Bridge. On the right is the Kelvin Hall and the Transport Museum (see **CHILDREN**, **A-Z**), and opposite is the Art Gallery & Museum (see **ART & CULTURE**, **A-Z**). Turn right into the museum grounds and walk around past the entrance facing away from the street, past the bowling greens on the right and join Kelvin Way. Turn left and walk down the pleasant tree-lined avenue. Halfway along, in a small diversion on the left, are statues of Lord Kelvin (see **A-Z**) and Baron Lister (1827-1912) the founder of antiseptic surgery. Re-enter the park on the right, the way you came out originally, and walk back over the bridge. Follow the path around to the right, past the fountain (1872) erected in memory of Robert Stewart, Lord Provost of Glasgow (1851-54) and follow the path straight ahead beside the playing fields and children's recreation area and out into Clairmont Gardens. Walk ahead and follow Woodside Place back to Charing Cross.

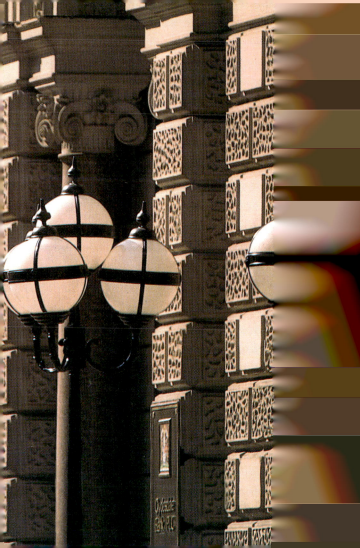

Accidents and Breakdowns: In the event of an accident find medical assistance for injured persons; inform the police; be sure to take the name, address, and insurance details of the other driver(s) involved, and the names, addresses and statements of any witnesses. Inform your insurance company as soon as possible.
Breakdowns: There are emergency telephones at regular intervals along motorways. Visitors who are members of motoring organizations in their own countries belonging to the International Touring Alliance can summon assistance free of charge from the Automobile Association (24-Hour Breakdown Service. Tel: 812 3999) and the Royal Automobile Association (24-Hour Rescue Service. Tel: 248 5474).

Accommodation: Glasgow offers a reasonable choice of accommodation in and around the city centre, including hotels, guesthouses, bed and breakfast establishments, self-catering apartments and a youth hostel. Accommodation is more expensive in the city centre than south of the river and in the west end.
According to the star rating system:
* good small hotels with simple facilities;
** offers a better standard of accommodation;
*** two-thirds of rooms have private bathrooms or showers;
**** high class hotels with superior accommodation and facilities.
Prices: The most expensive hotels charge around £70-£90 per person per night; medium priced hotels £30-£50 per person per night; the cheapest are £15-£20 per person. Guesthouses: £15 per person. Self-Catering: from £60-£250 per week. See **Youth Hostels**.
For more details and a comprehensive accommodation service contact the Tourist Information Centre, 35-39 St Vincent Place. Tel: 227 4880.

Airports: Glasgow is served by two main airports: Glasgow and Prestwick. Most European and domestic flights arrive at Glasgow Airport (tel: 887 1111) which is 13 km west of the city beside the M8 Motorway at junction 28. There are frequent bus and coach services to the city, and a coach/air link to Prestwick Airport. A taxi into the city centre will cost approximately £12. Transatlantic flights arrive at Prestwick Airport (tel: 0292 79822), 48 km south of the city. A regular

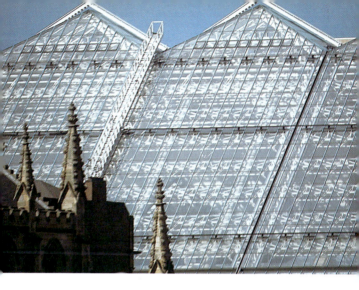

coach service runs to Glasgow, and a taxi costs around £35. Facilities at both airports include toilets, banks, shops, restaurants and bars.

Architecture: Glasgow possesses some of the finest examples of Victorian city architecture in Britain, but few buildings survive from earlier periods of its history. The important exception is the Gothic Cathedral (12thC onwards), the most notable historical and architectural site in the city (see **Glasgow Cathedral**). Provand's Lordship (1471) is a typical example of late medieval domestic design but is otherwise unremarkable. Only the steeples survive from the Tolbooth (1626) at Glasgow Cross (see **A-Z**) and Merchant's Hall (1665) in the Bridgegate, both once important buildings at the centre of the bustling 17thC Merchant City. The Georgian-style Cunninghame Mansion (1778) which lies at the heart of what is now Stirling's Library (see **A-Z**) and the Ionic columns and Venetian windows of Robert Adam's Trades House (1794) in Glassford Street are two notable buildings from the .

18thC, although both are obscured by later additions and insertions. The tower of St George's Tron Church (1807) in Buchanan Street, by William Stark, shows the influence of Wren and Hawksmoor. Another impressive site from the pre-Victorian period is David Hamilton's elegant Hutchesons' Hospital (1802-5) at 158 Ingram Street (see **A-Z**). He also designed the portico and cupola on Stirling's Library (1828-29). The magnificent legacy of public, commercial, religious and domestic architecture from the Victorian period reflects the city's pride and wealth during its heyday as the 'Second City of the Empire' and embraces an eclectic mix of styles: civic buildings such as the Renaissance-style City Chambers (1883-88) by William Young (see **A-Z**); commercial buildings like William Leiper's Templeton's Business Centre (1889), modelled on a Venetian Palace, with its unique and exotic display of coloured brickwork (see **A-Z**); John Burnet's Baroque Clydesdale Bank (1870-73) at 30-40 St Vincent's Place (see **WALK 2**); Alexander 'Greek' Thomson's St Vincent Street Church (1858), distinctive and unorthodox with its Italianate towers (see **WALK 2**); Sir Gilbert Scott's Gothic-style Glasgow University building (1866-70) on Gilmorehill. Charles Wilson's Park Circus (1855) has been described as the 'grandest town planning exercise in mid-Victorian Britain'; it and the grand terraces of the west end reflect the wealth and self-confidence of Victorian suburbia (for the University and west end see **WALK 3**). Tenement designs are also of interest: see for example the decorative facade of Charing Cross Mansions (1891) at the end of Sauchiehall Street (see **WALK 2**). The most famous architect associated with the city is of course Charles Rennie Mackintosh, whose work was a reaction to this Victorian eclecticism, a unique fusion of national historical forms and modernism. His buildings often bemused his contemporaries, but today they are among the city's most precious assets (see **MACKINTOSH, A-Z**).

Argyle Street: One of the leading shopping thoroughfares in the city. Named after the Duke of Argyle whose funeral procession passed down the street in 1761.

Argyll Arcade: Glasgow's original glass-covered shopping precinct with iron-framed hammerbeam roof designed by John Baird (1827). It runs from Argyle Street to Buchanan Street and is packed with gold-smiths, silversmiths, jewellers and diamond merchants. See **SHOPPING 1**.

Babysitters: Hotels, guesthouses and some bed and breakfast accommodation will provide a child-minding service, but there is no centrally organized service for the city as a whole.

Banks: See **Money**.

Barras, The: Glasgow's famous weekend market in the east of the city is an institution with a special charm all of its own. There are over 800 stalls selling anything and everything. The market is mostly cov-ered but also spills out into the surrounding streets and the area has some lively pubs, cafés and street entertainment too. See **SHOPPING 1**.

Best Buys: Tweeds, tartan and knitwear are cheaper than in Edinburgh. See **SHOPPING 1**.

Bicycle Hire: Contact: Tor-Toys, 193 Clarkston Rd (tel: 637 2439) and 1417 Dumbarton Road (tel: 958 1055) - £5 per day, £8 two days and £20 per week; Dales (Cycles) Ltd, 150 Dobbies Loan (tel: 332 2705) hire only by the week for around £30; and the Youth Hostel, 10 Woodlands Terrace (tel: 332 3004) - summer hire only. See **SPORTS** for details of the Loch Lomond Cycle Route.

Blythswood Square: Designed by John Brash and laid out in the 1820s when the city began its 19thC expansion westwards. The square is now a prestigious business address. The east side is occupied by the Royal Scottish Automobile Club and is the starting point for the annual International Scottish Rally in June. Mackintosh designed the doorway of No. 5 which used to be the headquarters of the Glasgow Society of Lady Artists. No. 7 was once the home of Madeleine Smith (see **A-Z**). The architectural features of the square are now somewhat spoilt by the numerous cars parked around the central gardens, which are them-selves rather wild and overgrown. See **WALK 2**.

Botanic Gardens: A beautiful park on the banks of the Kelvin, once owned by the Royal Botanical Institute of Glasgow and transferred to the city in 1891. It has linked conservatories housing a variety of tropical plants and orchids, and the famous Kibble Palace, a magnificent Victorian glasshouse with ornamental ponds, Victorian sculptures and a valuable collection of tree ferns and South American and Asian flora. See **PARKS**.

Broomielaw: The area between Argyle Street and the river was the site of the first quay built on the Clyde in 1662, although the river did not become navigable up to the city until the late 18thC. The launching of Henry Bell's *Comet* in 1812 heralded the development of regular steamship passenger services on the Clyde and fifty years later, at the height of the summer trade, up to 40 or 50 steamers a day, with names such as the *Iona, Columba* or the *Duchess of Rothesay* used to leave the Broomielaw for the Clyde resorts favoured by hordes of Glaswegians for their annual holidays. Those days are long gone but nostalgia for the Clyde steamers and trips 'doon the watter' remains strong, and those pleasures can still be experienced with a trip on the *Waverley* (see **CHILDREN**). See **Clyde**.

Buchanan Street: A pedestrian precinct and important shopping area also popular with street entertainers. In the late 18thC it formed the western boundary of the city. Note the impressive Clydesdale Bank (1896) at the corner of Gordon Street, which was originally designed as a tearoom by the Edinburgh architect Washington Browne. The north of the street is undergoing major redevelopment with the construction of a new concert hall and shopping centre which are due to open in 1990.

Budget:

	High	Low
Accommodation per person (incl.breakfast)	£90	£15
Lunch/snack	£12	£5
Dinner (for two)	£30	£15
Museum	Free	
Theatre (for two)	£16	£6
Taxi	£10	£1.50
Bus	£1.20	30p
Brandy	£1.50	90p
Wine (glass)	£1.30	90p

Burns, Robert: Arguably Scotland's greatest poet and certainly the best-loved by ordinary Scots. He was born in Alloway, Ayrshire on 25 January 1759, educated locally and began to write poems while still at school. After the death of his father in 1784 he took over the ailing family farm but found it hard to make a living, and the famous Kilmarnock Edition of his poems (July 1786) was published to try to alleviate his financial difficulties. The edition earned him only £20, but it also conferred instant fame and in 1786 he headed for Edinburgh, where he was lauded by literary society and involved himself in a number of amorous adventures. He also made frequent visits to Glasgow during 1786-7, but his satirical humour at the expense of the clerical establishment was not as well received here as in the capital. As well as writing poetry he collected and wrote over 200 songs such as *Auld Lang Syne*, *Ye Banks and Braes* and *O my luve's like a red, red rose*. In June 1788 he took up the lease of Ellisland, a farm near Dumfries, and married Jean Armour but he was again unsuccessful as a farmer, and in 1789 he moved to Dumfries and became an excise officer at £50 a year. In 1791 he published his last major poem, and his best known - *Tam O'Shanter*. He died five years later. His birthday, 'Burns Night', 25 January, is celebrated all over the world. See **EXCURSION 1**.

Burrell, William (1861-1958): Sir William Burrell was a wealthy Victorian shipping magnate with a talent for making money and a passion for collecting works of art. His interests ranged from the ancient art of Mediterranean civilizations to late Gothic and medieval tapestries, furniture, sculpture and stained glass; Japanese prints; and 19thC French painting. In 1927 he was knighted for his services to art, and in

1944 he gifted his collection to the city. Burrell wanted the collection to be exhibited in a rural setting, and it was not until 1967, when Pollok Estate was presented to the city, that a home for the collection was agreed upon. The award-winning sandstone and glass-walled gallery building was opened in 1983 and is designed to complement the individual exhibits and natural surroundings to the full.
Burrell Collection, Pollok Country Park, Pollokshaws Rd, 1000-1700 Mon.-Sat., 1400-1700 Sun. Free. See **BURRELL**.

Buses: Strathclyde Buses is the largest operator, their distinctive orange buses covering the whole of the city. Services run from 0600-2330 (night buses leave from George Square 0030, 0145, 0300, 0415 to various destinations throughout the city). The exact fare is required. Other companies (blue or red buses) compete on similar routes (exact fare not required). Unless indicated, all bus numbers given for destinations throughout this guide refer to orange buses.
Buchanan Bus Station, Killermont St. (tel: 332 9644) provides local services to the north and east of the city, and coach services to a large number of Scottish and English cities including Edinburgh and London. From Anderston Bus Station, Argyle St. (tel: 248 7432) buses leave for the south of the city, Calderpark Zoo, south-west Scotland and the Clyde resorts. Contact the Travel Centre, St Enoch Square (0900-1700 Mon.-Sat. Tel: 226 4826) for all Underground, bus, rail, and ferry information in Strathclyde.

Cameras and Photography: All makes of film are available in camera shops, chemists and department stores, and many shops also provide a fast one-day developing service: Tom Dickson Cameras, 15/17 Queen St.; Dixons, 48 Argyle St.; Foto Machine, 63 Renfield St.

Camping and Caravanning: Barnbrock Camping Site, Barnbrock Farm, Kilbarchan, Renfrewshire. Tel: (0505) 690915; £1.85 per night two persons/tent; room for 15 tents.
Hogganfield Caravan Site, 1563 Cumbernauld Road, Millerston. Tel: 770 5602, evenings 776 3020; £4.00 per night. Touring pitches: ten caravans, four motor caravans.

Kilmardinny Riding Centre, Milngavie Road, Bearsden. Tel: 942 4404; £3.00 per night per caravan; £2.80 per night for tents. Touring pitches: ten caravans, ten motor caravans, 15 tents.
Craigendmuir Caravan Park, Campsie View, Stepps Glasgow. Tel: 779 2973; £3.50 per night car and caravan. Touring pitches: 14 touring and six motor caravans.

Car Hire: All you need to rent a car is a valid driving licence. Rates are around £120-£150 per week or £25-£30 per day for a small family car with unlimited mileage all-inclusive of insurance and Value Added Tax. The minimum age for hiring a vehicle is 21 (Avis is 23) and you must have at least one year's driving experience.
Avis, 161 North St. Tel: 221 2827.
Arnold Clark, St Georges House, St Georges Road, Charing Cross. Tel: 332 2626.
Hertz Rent-A-Car, St Andrews Drive, Abbotsinch Airport, Paisley. Tel: 887 2451 & 106 Waterloo St., Tel: 248 7736.
Budget Rent-A-Car, 101 Waterloo St. Tel: 226 4141/2.
Mitchell's Self Drive, Mitchell St. Tel: 221 8461.
Swan National, 222 Broomielaw. Tel: 204 1051.

Celtic: Founded in 1888 to raise funds for the poor in the city's east end. The team has enjoyed major successes in the international football scene, and the fierce rivalry between Celtic and Glasgow Rangers when the two meet in 'Old Firm' games is part of the fabric of Glasgow life. With the exception of Hampden Park, home of the second division amateur side Queen's Park, Celtic Park is the largest club ground in Britain. 95 Kerrydale Street. Bus Nos 62, 64 from Argyle St. See **Ibrox**.

Chemists: Boots The Chemists, Boots Corner, Union St., tel: 248 7387; Sundays and late opening: Sinclair Pharmacy, 693 Great Western Road. 0900-2100 daily, tel: 339 0012; C. M. Mackie, 1067 Pollokshaws Rd. 0900-2000 Mon.-Fri., 0900-1800 Sat., 1100-1800 Sun., tel: 649 8915. For emergency prescriptions overnight or at week-ends contact the police. See **Emergencies**, **Health**, **Police**.

Children: In fine weather you can always amuse children with an outing to one of the many parks dotted in and around the city (see **PARKS**); in wet weather, however, it is more difficult to keep them entertained. The Transport Museum, Haggs Castle, Calderpark Zoo and the Pollok Leisure Pool are all of particular interest for children. Most restaurants are happy to accommodate families, but the more expensive ones may prohibit young toddlers. Most pubs will not allow children on the premises, although a few do make provision for families especially when food is being ordered. See **CHILDREN**.

Cigarettes and Tobacco: Most brands are available and normally sold in packs of ten or 20 in newsagents, hotels, restaurants and pubs; vending machines may dispense packs of 17 or 18 depending on the brand. Price is around £1.50 for 20. Many brands of pipe and cigarette tobacco are also widely available, most commonly in half-ounce (around £1.20) and one-ounce packs or pouches.
Specialist tobacconist: Graham Robert & Co, 71 St Vincent St.
See **Smoking**.

City Chambers: A beautiful building designed by William Young in Italian Renaissance style (1883-8). The interior and exterior are lavishly ornamented; the loggia - or entrance hall - with its polished granite columns supporting a vaulted ceiling and domes covered with Venetian mosaic is in the style of a Renaissance Roman church; a magnificent marble staircase leads up to the semi-circular Council Hall with a central dome decorated with stained glass, panelled walls in Spanish mahogany, public gallery, distinguished visitors' gallery and Press area. The Satinwood Salon, adjoining Octagonal Room with amber wood panelling, and the Mahogany Salon contain paintings on loan from the Art Gallery. The walls of the Banqueting Hall are covered with panels depicting episodes from the history of the city. The whole represents the power and prestige of Victorian Glasgow and should not be missed. George Square. Guided tours 1030 and 1430 Mon., Tues., Wed., and Fri. (except when the council is in session). Free. See **WALK 1**.

Climate: Glasgow, along with the west coast of Scotland, is generally warmer and wetter than Edinburgh and the east coast. The average temperature in January is 3.2 °C, and it can get much colder during the winter months. In July the average temperature is 17 °C, but summers are often disappointingly dull and wet. The weather can be very changeable, and it is advisable to bring warm jumpers and coats as well as light clothing.

Clyde: The Clyde, with its estuary and convenient access to the Atlantic and North America, has played a crucial role in the economic history of Glasgow. Until the late18thC, the river at Glasgow was too shallow for ships to sail up to the city (in 1750 the depth of the river at the Broomielaw was only 40 cm), and the main sources of Glasgow's prosperity in the 18thC - sugar (for rum), cotton and tobacco - were imported from America to Port Glasgow further down the river and carried to the city on carts or small rowing boats. With the development of steamships in the early 19thC, the quay at the Broomielaw was extended and the river widened and deepened so that large vessels could gain access to the city. Growth in the Clyde valley coal mining and iron industry at the same period led to a rapid expansion in shipbuilding on the Clyde, new methods of construction were pioneered, and by the late 19thC Glasgow was established as the centre of shipbuilding and marine and heavy engineering in Britain. Passenger liners (the *Queen Mary* (1934) was perhaps the greatest ever built), merchant ships and naval vessels were produced in their thousands - the label 'Clyde-built' was revered as a mark of excellence and Glasgow was known as the 'Second City of the Empire'. Today the shipyards are largely silent after years of decline due to stagnation in world demand and competition

from more efficient producers. The city has paid a heavy price in terms of unemployment and social deprivation, but a new spirit of optimism for the future is enthusing Glaswegians; the docklands and shipyards are being developed for new housing and leisure activities, and the city is entering a new era of self-confidence, symbolized by its nomination as City of Culture 1990. See **Broomielaw**.

Complaints: Greater Glasgow Tourist Board, 35-39 St Vincent Place. Tel: 227 4880. Glasgow District Council Public Relations Department, City Chambers, George Square. Tel: 227 4157/8/9. Strathclyde Regional Council Headquarters, 20 India St. Tel: 204 2900. Citizens' Advice Bureau, 212 Bath St. Tel: 331 2345. National Trust for Scotland, Hutchesons' Hospital, 158 Ingram St. Tel: 552 8391.

Consulates: Australia: Hobart House, 80 Hanover St., Edinburgh. Tel: 031-226 6271. Canada: 151 St Vincent St. Tel: 221 4415. USA: 3 Regent Terrace, Edinburgh. Tel: 031 556 8315.

Conversion Charts:

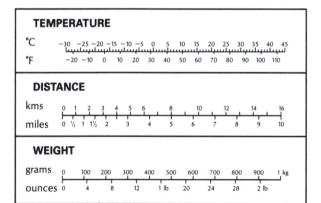

Credit Cards: See **Money**.

Crime and Theft: Glasgow is a friendly city, and there is very little street crime, but it is wise to take all the normal precautions against petty criminals and opportunist thieves, so make sure your car is locked, beware of pickpockets and keep a firm hold of your camera, handbag, and other valuables. If you do have something stolen tell a police officer or go to the nearest police station. See **Police**.

Crookston Castle: A ruined 15thC tower-house built by the Stewarts of Darnley, where Mary Queen of Scots and Henry, Lord Darnley lodged after their marriage in 1565. Only the north east tower, originally one of four, remains intact. 1000-1900 Mon.-Sat., 1400-1900 Sun. (Apr.-Sept.); 1000-1600 Mon.-Sat., 1400-1600 Sun. (Oct.-Mar.). Free. South west of Glasgow off the A 736.

Currency: Scottish bank notes come in denominations of £50, £20, £10 and £5 and are issued by the Bank of Scotland, the Royal Bank of Scotland and the Clydesdale Bank; unlike in England, there is still a £1 note. Coins are divided into £1, 50p, 20p, 10p, 5p, 2p, and 1p units. A 10p piece is the minimum charge in phone boxes. Scottish notes of large denomination may be treated with some suspicion in England so it is advisable to exchange them for English notes before travelling south of the border. See **Money**.

Customs:

Duty Paid Into:	Cigarettes	or	Cigars	or	Tobacco	Spirits	Wine
E.E.C.	300		75		400 g	1.5 *l*	5 *l*
U.K.	300		75		400 g	1.5 *l*	5 *l*

Dentists: See **Health**.

Disabled: Many tourist attractions, theatres, restaurants and bars can accommodate the disabled, as can some public transport. For more details contact the Tourist Information Centre, 35-39 St Vincent Place. Tel: 227 4880.

Doctors: See **Health**.

Drinks: Tea is more popular than coffee, although continental-style cappuccino and espresso are readily available in the city centre and west end, less so elsewhere. Whisky is the traditional Scottish drink; try one of the malts, pale unblended spirits which are more expensive but are a class above blended varieties. There are three main varieties of local beer: Heavy, which is a draught beer with a slightly bitter taste: Export, which is stronger and darker; and Special, similar to Heavy. Real ales (cask-fermented and pumped to the taps naturally, without using carbon dioxide) such as Belhaven, Greenmantle, Theakston and others can be found in various city bars. American and continental lagers such as Budweiser, Red Stripe, Grolsch and Furstenburg have become increasingly favoured over local brands such as Tennents. Guinness, which is strong and heavily malted with a distinctive dark body and thick creamy head, is also popular. The price of a pint of heavy or export is around £1. Ordinary lager is slightly more expensive at around £1.20, Continental brands can be up to £1.50, real ales and Guinness are also around £1.50 a pint. Wine by the glass (about £1) or bottle is also widely available, and fashionable wine bars and bistros are now among the most popular places for drinking. Few Glaswegians (especially women) lament the passing of the old-style Glasgow drinking dens for which the city was once infamous, although some traditional pubs are the best in the city (see **PUBS**). It is illegal to sell alcohol to those under 18; few pubs will allow children inside, although some make special provision with designated family areas. Alcoholic drinks can also be purchased at off-licences, which are usually open 0900-2200 Mon.-Sat., and most pubs will sell alcohol over the bar to 'carry out', although they charge more. See **Opening Times**.

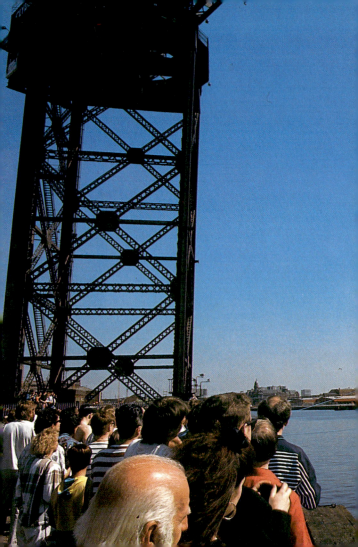

Driving: Possession of a valid driving licence is required to drive on British roads. Drive on the left and overtake on the right, at junctions and roundabouts give way to traffic from the right. The speed limit is 110 kmph (70 mph) on motorways, 95 kmph (60 mph) on other roads and 45 kmph (30mph) or 65 kmph (40 mph) in urban areas. Seat belts are compulsory and there are stiff penalties for drinking and driving. Road signs are similar to other countries. There is a confusing one-way system in the centre of Glasgow which can make driving a frustrating experience. Parking in the city centre can also be difficult and costly; there are 24-hour multi-storey car parks at Anderston Cross, George Street, Mitchell Street and Waterloo Street; the cheapest car park in the centre is in the St Enoch Centre. Some streets have parking meters (20p per 40 min). There are £12 fines for illegal parking (eg. on double yellow lines) and traffic wardens and the police patrol the streets regularly on the look-out for offenders. Parking restrictions are relaxed in the evenings and at weekends, but it is advisable to take advantage of the parking facilities available at Bridge Street, Kelvinbridge, Shields Road and West Street Underground stations so you can 'Park and Ride' into the city centre without hassle. See **Accidents and Breakdowns**, **Petrol**.

Drugs: There are heavy penalties for possession of drugs so beware.

Eating Out: There are a substantial variety of eating places in the city ranging from expensive restaurants (£25 per head for dinner) serving continental-style haute cuisine and modern Scottish dishes, to moderately priced establishments (£10-£15 per head) serving Italian, Indian and Chinese food. There are also a number of stylish cafés, fashionable pubs and wine bars which serve food all day and these are the places for good inexpensive meals in the city centre (£5-£10 per head). If you are feeling romantic you can also enjoy a candlelit dinner cruise on the Clyde. Glasgow also has the usual complement of fast-food outlets such as pizzerias, fish and chip shops, hamburger joints and kebab houses scattered throughout the city. See PUBS, RESTAURANTS.

Electricity: The standard voltage is 240 Volts AC; plugs have three square pins; fuses are 3, 5, or 13 amps. To use non-standard electrical appliances you will need a suitable adaptor.

Emergencies: Dial 999 (no money is needed) and state whether the police, an ambulance or the fire brigade is required. See **Accidents and Breakdowns**, **Crime and Theft**, **Health**.

Events: Glasgow plays host to a regular series of art, music and drama festivals, and in recent years the city has seriously challenged Edinburgh's claim to be the cultural capital of Scotland.
February: Festival of Music, Speech and Dance at Pollok.
May: The Mayfest (see **A-Z**).

June: SNO Proms; Lord Provost's Procession; Flower Festival in Glasgow Cathedral; Glasgow Show; Jazz Festival.
July: Folk Festival; Street Entertainment Festival; Carnival on Glasgow Green.
August: World Pipe Band Championship, Bellahouston Park; Royal Scottish Automobile Club Veteran and Vintage Car Run.
September: Glasgow Marathon.

November: Glasgow Tryst (Scottish Music).
December: Pantomimes; Carnival at the SECC.
For more details contact the Tourist Information Centre, 35-39 St
Vincent Place. Tel: 227 4880.

Food: The most famous Scottish dish is haggis, a mixture of minced
heart, lungs, oatmeal, suet, onions and seasonings boiled in a sheep's
stomach-bag. It sounds disgusting, but is actually quite tasty and is usually served in the traditional manner with mashed potatoes and turnip,
known as 'Haggis and neeps'. Porridge for breakfast (taken with salt,
not sugar!) is another Scottish tradition, as is the substantial cooked
breakfast comprising egg, bacon, sausage (in square slices), black pud-
ding and potato ('tattie') scones. Oatcakes are another Scots delicacy,
usually served with butter and jam, or cheese. Oatmeal is also used as
a coating for herrings, and other tasty fish dishes found on menus
include Loch Fyne Kippers, Arbroath Smokies and Finnan Haddies
(smoked haddock). Hot and substantial soups like Scotch broth and
Cock-a-Leekie (chicken stock with vegetables and prunes) are also popular menu items. 'Scotch Pies' or 'Mutton Pies' (chewy pastry cases
filled with minced lamb) are another local speciality. Of course those
with more delicate and expensive palates will relish the plentiful supply
of fresh salmon, trout, lobster, venison, Scotch lamb, Aberdeen Angus
beef and game such as hare, pheasant, partridge and grouse served in
the choicer restaurants in and around the city.
See **RESTAURANTS**.

George Square: In the heart of the city. The square was laid out in
1781 and named in honour of George III. On the east side are the City
Chambers (see **A-Z**) and facing them on the west side is the Merchants'
House. The 24 m high fluted column is a memorial to Sir Walter Scott
(1771-1832), Scotland's greatest novelist, and was erected in 1837.
Among the floral displays are various statues including Queen Victoria
(reigned 1837-1901) and her consort Prince Albert; poet Robert Burns
(1759-96); 19thC Prime Minister William E. Gladstone (1809-98) and
the engineer James Watt (1736-1819). The Cenotaph by John Burnet
commemorates the dead of two World Wars. See **WALK 1**.

Glasgow Cathedral: One of the most important and historic buildings in the city. Built in Gothic 'First Pointed' style, the Cathedral is best viewed from the Necropolis above (see **A-Z**). The earliest church on this spot was founded by St Mungo (see **A-Z**) on the site of a Christian burial ground consecrated by St Ninian in the 5thC. The first stone church was founded by Bishop Achaius and King David I in 1136, and rebuilt (after a fire) in 1197 although little remains of the original. The present building was begun by Bishop William de Bondington (1233-1258) and completed by Archbishop Robert Blacader (1483-1508). The Lower Church (crypt), Choir and Tower were completed in the 13thC. The interior is very impressive (if rather gloomy) and resonant with history, although the church is still used for worship. The Upper Church comprises the nave and choir and aside from the magnificent architecture other items worth noting are the stained glass West Window, the 15thC quire screen east of the nave and the array of Scottish regimental colours. The Lower Church contains the Blacader Aisle (15thC), the memorial to the Covenanters executed at Glasgow Cross in 1636, the tomb of St Mungo and a series of small side-chapels. The Cathedral Precinct at the entrance is being redeveloped and a new Visitors'

Centre containing a tourist shop, museum, restaurant and snack-bar is planned to open in 1990. Castle St. 15 minutes' walk north east of George Square.
0930-1230,1330-1600 Mon.-Sat., 1400-1600 Sun. Oct.-Mar.
0930-1300, 1400-1900 Mon.-Sat., 1400-1700 Sun. Apr.-Sept.
Sunday Services 1100 & 1830; all welcome.

Glasgow Cross: At the foot of the High Street; the heart of the city in the 17th and 18thC. The only surviving part of the 17thC Tolbooth - or Town House - where the Tobacco Lords used to meet is the Steeple (1626). Close by is the Mercat Cross, designed in 1920s to replace the original which marked the site of a market held in the city from medieval times.

Glasgow Green: The oldest, best-loved and most popular park in the city, it has had a long and varied history at the centre of public life as the scene of political gatherings, parades, and exhibitions. It contains the People's Palace (see **A-Z**) and beside it the Winter Gardens (1898) with exotic plants and tearoom. Overlooking the park is the distinctive Templeton's Business Centre, a former carpet factory (see **A-Z**). Nelson's column was erected in 1807 (predating the famous London monument), and nearby is a plaque commemorating James Watt's idea for an improved design of steam engine conceived during a stroll here in 1765 (see **Watt**). The earthenware Doulton Fountain with the statue of Queen Victoria is named after the famous china manuacturer. The Green has been rather neglected in recent years and there are plans to landscape and renovate the whole area. See PARKS, WALK 1.

Guides: The Scottish Tourist Guides Association can provide fully-trained guides proficient in most European languages for group or individual tours around the city. Contact the Secretary, Mrs Jan Philip. Tel: 776 1052.

Haggs Castle Museum: Dating from 1585, and originally built as the residence of the Maxwell family, the castle is now a museum with a 16thC kitchen, Victorian nursery, and temporary exhibition areas

Tollcross

61

Strathclyde's Buses

NO CHANGE
given on this bus

ATLANTEAN

XUS 621S

LA 1250

organized to help children understand and appreciate the past through activities such as making butter, weaving, baking, dancing and dressing up in period costumes. For further information contact the Museum Education Officer, tel: 334 1131. See **CHILDREN**.

Hairdressers: Vidal Sassoon, Princes Square. Tel: 226 4484; Rita Rusk, 49 West Nile St. Tel: 221 1472. Harold Kramer, 65 Queen St. Tel: 248 4008. The Hely Hair Studio, 342 Sauchiehall St. Tel: 332 6068. Taylor Ferguson, 106 Bath St. Tel: 332 0397.

Health: Be sure to take out full health insurance before you travel and to bring any prescription drugs you use with you, and a note from your doctor for customs officers. All hospitals will treat emergency cases. Citizens of EC countries and some others can receive free care from the National Health Service for all accidents, emergencies and infectious diseases. You must pay if you are hospitalized for non-emergency treatment so insurance is essential. Chemists will charge £2.60 for prescriptions issued by a doctor.
Emergency Dental Service: Glasgow Dental Hospital, 378 Sauchiehall St. Tel: 332 7020.
Hospitals:
Glasgow Royal Infirmary, 82-84 Castle St. Tel:552 3535
Royal Alexandra Infirmary, Barbour Park, Neilston Road, Paisley. Tel: 887 9111
Royal Hospital for Sick Children, Yorkhill. Tel: 339 8888
Southern General Hospital, 1345 Govan Road. Tel: 445 2466
Stobhill General Hospital, 133 Balornock Road. Tel: 558 0111
Victoria Infirmary, Grange Road, Langside. Tel: 339 8822
Western Infirmary, Dumbarton Road. Tel: 339 8822

Hospitals: See previous entry.

Hutchesons' Hospital: Elegant classical building designed by David Hamilton in 1802 to house the charitable hospital and school originally established in the Trongate in 1641 by George and Thomas Hutcheson. Statues of the brothers (by James Coquhoun, 1649) stand in

two niches in the facade. It's now the regional office of the National Trust for Scotland with a Visitor Centre and gift shop.
158 Ingram St. (on the corner of John St.). 0900-1700 Mon.-Fri., 1000-1600 Sat. Free. Tel: 552 8391.

Ibrox Football Stadium: One of the most modern and impressive stadiums in Britain, and the home of Glasgow Rangers Football Club founded on Glasgow Green in 1873. To visit the Trophy Room contact the Secretary, Edmiston Drive. Tel: 427 5232. U Ibrox. See **Celtic**.

Information: Greater Glasgow Tourist Board, 35-39 St Vincent Place (tel: 227 4880), provides Information Sheets listing eating places, pubs, tourist attractions, sporting facilities and lots more. Also maps of the city, currency exchange, an accommodation service, tours, events and what's on.
The British Tourist Authority can provide information on Scotland at the following addresses:
Australia: Associated Midland House, 171 Clarence St., Sydney, N.S.W. 2000. Tel: 02-29 8627.
Canada: Suite 600, 94 Cumberland St., Toronto, Ontario M5R 3N3. Tel: 416-925 6326
Ireland: 123 Lr Baggot St., Dublin 2. Tel: 01-614188
New Zealand: 8th Floor, Norwich Union Building, Cnr Queen & Durham Streets, Auckland. Tel: 09-31446.
USA: Chicago: John Hancock Centre, Suite 3320, 875 N. Michigan Avenue, Chicago, IL 60611. Tel: 312-787 0490.
Dallas: Cedar Maple Plaza, Suite 210, 2305 Cedar Springs Road, Dallas, TX 75201. Tel: 214-720 4040.
Los Angeles: World Trade Centre, Suite 450, 350 South Figueroa St., Los Angeles, CA 90071. Tel: 213-623 8196.
New York: 40 West 57th St., New York, NY 10019. Tel: 212-581 4700.

Kelvin, William Thomson (1824-1907): Professor of Physics at Glasgow University for 53 years. He was a mathematical genius and graduated from the University at the age of ten. He went on to Cambridge, worked in France for a brief period and was appointed to

the Chair of Natural Philosophy at Glasgow when he was 22. A brilliant theoretician, he could also devise practical and financially profitable applications arising from his researches: he invented the submarine cable for transatlantic telegraph transmission, and devoted much time to the improvement of scientific instrumentation, including the development of the first electric meter - his home was the first to be lit by electric light. The epitome of the practical Scot, there is a statue of him in Kelvin Way. See **WALK 3**.

Kelvingrove Art Gallery and Museum: The red sandstone building on the banks of the Kelvin was opened to the public in 1902. It has 20 galleries grouped around two side courts and a central hall. There are displays covering Natural History, Archaeology, History, Ethnography, Weapons and Armour, and Decorative and Fine Art. Paintings embrace works from all the major European Schools including Dutch 17thC masters, the Impressionists, and British works from 17th-20thC. Scottish art, including the 'Glasgow Boys', is given particular emphasis. One of the most popular works with visitors is Dali's *Christ of St John of the Cross.* There is a shop, coffee bar, free guide service and organ recitals on Saturday afternoons in summer. See **ART & CULTURE**, **WALK 3**.

Kelvingrove Park: On the banks of the River Kelvin close to the University and Art Gallery, it was designed by Joseph Paxton and Charles Wilson in 1854 for the use of prosperous Victorian westenders. It was the site of the great International Exhibitions of 1888, 1901 and 1911, which helped to finance the Art Gallery and Museum building (see previous entry). The 85 acres of parkland includes various statues and memorials, the Stewart Fountain, duck pond, open-air concert area, skateboard arena and recreation park. See **PARKS**, **WALK 3**.

Laundries: 20 Osborne St., near Glasgow Cross (self-service only, £2). Tel: 552 4219; Majestic Launderette, 1110 Argyle St. Tel: 339 6530; Dry Cleaners: Munro, 277 Sauchiehall St. Tel: 332 6815; Swiss Cleaners,164a Buchanan St. Tel: 332 3396; J. Pullar & Sons, 89 Mitchell St. Tel: 248 7824.

Lost Property: For Strathclyde Buses and the Glasgow Underground inquire at the St Enoch Lost Property Office, St Enoch Underground Station 0900-1645 Mon.-Fri. Tel: 248 6950.
Other buses: inquiries to Buchanan Bus Station 0630-2215 daily. Tel: 332 6950. Anderston Bus Station 0800-1700 Mon.-Sat. Tel: 248 7432.
Rail: Central Station 0630-2300 Mon.-Sat., 0730-2300 Sun. Tel: 332 9822 ext. 4362. Queen St. Station 0700-2200 Mon.-Fri., 0700-2000 Sat. Tel: 332 9811 ext. 3276.
Air: Glasgow Airport lost property desk. Tel: 887 1111 ext. 4558.
City: Strathclyde Police Headquarters, Central Lost Property Office, 173 Pitt St. Tel: 204 2626.

Mackintosh, Charles Rennie (1868-1928): Architect, designer and water-colourist, the most celebrated figure in the 'Glasgow Style' movement (a variation on Art Nouveau) which flourished during the period 1890-1920; a cult figure now, he was relatively neglected during his own lifetime. He was born in Glasgow in 1868, the son of a police superintendent. In 1884 he began his professional training and also enrolled in classes at the art school where he became the leading

figure among a number of accomplished designers and artists. By 1900, when he married Margaret Macdonald (also a talented designer and water colourist), he had already established his credentials as a gifted architect, achieved recognition through exhibitions in Europe and had designed his greatest building, the School of Art (1897-1909): the first European building in the 'modern style' and a landmark in architectural history. His other major buildings include Queen's Cross Church (1897-99), Windyhill in Kilmacolm (1899), Hill House in Helensburgh (1902-4), the Willow Tearooms (1903) and Scotland Street School (1904), but after 1905 few new commissions were forthcoming and dis-illusioned with Glasgow, he left the city in 1913 never to return. The Mackintoshes settled in Chelsea in 1915, and concentrated mainly on designing printed fabrics and watercolour painting. In 1923 they retired to Port Vendres in the South of France. Suffering from cancer, Mackintosh returned to London in 1927 and died on 10 December 1928. See MACKINTOSH.

Mayfest: For three weeks in May, Glasgow plays host to an international festival of the arts, embracing theatre, music, dance and fringe comedy in numerous venues throughout the city. Contact Mayfest, 46 Royal Exchange Square for details. Tel: 221 4911.

McLellan Galleries: Originally housed the art collection of Archibald McLellan (1796-1854) coach-builder, which was acquired by the city in 1856 and became the foundation of the city's municipal collection now housed in the Kelvingrove Art Gallery. The building was later extended and was used for miscellaneous exhibitions of arts and crafts, and as centre for political meetings and debate. It was seriously damaged by fire in 1988, and has now been restored and converted into an international exhibition venue. Sauchiehall St. on the corner with Rose St. See WALK 2.

Merchant City: The area south and east of George Square between Virginia St. and Candleriggs - the commercial hub of the city in the 18thC. The area became rather shabby in the 1960s and 1970s but has been revitalized and is now a desirable residential area with refurbished housing, the Candleriggs Market, fashionable bars, restaurants and boutiques.

Mitchell Library: Established in 1874 under the bequest of tobacco merchant Stephen Mitchell, the library was first opened in Ingram St. and then Miller St., and is now housed in the copper-domed building built in 1907-11. It is the largest civic-owned reference library in Europe and its stock of over one million books includes an extensive collection of Burns and Scottish literature. The west side of the building in Granville St. houses the Mitchell Theatre.
North St., near Charing Cross. 0930-2100 Mon., Tues., Thurs., Fri.; 0930-1700 Sat. Free. See WALK 2.

Money: The main banks in the city centre include:
Bank of England, 25 St Vincent Place. Tel: 221 4153
Bank of Ireland, 19 St Vincent Place. Tel: 221 9353
Bank of Scotland, 110 St Vincent St. Tel: 221 7071
Clydesdale Bank, 30 St Vincent Place. Tel: 248 7070
Co-operative Bank, 47 St Vincent St. Tel: 248 3388

Lloyds Bank, 12 Bothwell St. Tel: 248 4661
National Westminster Bank, 14 Blythswood Square. Tel: 221 6981
Royal Bank of Scotland, 98 Buchanan St. Tel: 248 2777
Trustee Savings Bank, 177 Ingram St.. Tel: 552 6244
Saturday opening: Barclays Bank, 90 St Vincent St. Tel: 221 9585; TSB,
9-11 Renfield St. 0930-1600. Tel: 204 1286.
Credit Cards: All the major cards are accepted by hotels, restaurants,
shops and garages in Glasgow, including Access (Mastercard),
American Express, Diners Club, Eurocard and Visa. Traveller's cheques
are a safe and convenient way to carry money and they can be cashed
at banks (which offer the best exchange rates), post offices, hotels,
restaurants and independent bureaux de change, including:
Thomas Cook, 15 Gordon St. 0900-1715 Mon., Tues., Thurs., Fri.;
0930-1715 Wed.; 0900-1600 Sat. Tel: 221 9431.
A T Mays, 90 Queen St. 0900-1730 Mon.-Fri., 0900-1700 Sat. Tel: 221
0404/6048.
American Express, 115 Hope St. 0900-1700 Mon.-Fri., 0900-1200 Sat.
Tel: 226 3077.
Central Station, Gordon St. 0800-2000. Tel: 226 5100.
Queen St. Station 0700-2300. Tel: 332 9811.
See **Currency**, **Opening Times**.

Music: Glasgow has a lot to offer music lovers, from opera buffs to
aficionados of modern jazz. The Scottish National Orchestra under its
conductor Neeme Jarvi performs regularly at the City Halls (a more
modern concert hall will open soon in Buchanan St.) and is one of
Britain's finest orchestras. Scottish Opera was founded in 1962 by
Alexander Gibson, the city's favourite musical son (who also led the
SNO for many years) and presents world-class performances in the
Theatre Royal, Scotland's only opera house. The Theatre Royal is also
used by the Scottish Ballet (founded 1969), a first-class company which
has toured all over the world. Chamber music, too, is strongly repre-
sented, with the Scottish Chamber Orchestra, Scottish Early Music
Consort and Cantilena. The city also boasts many fine choirs such as
the Glasgow Orpheus Choir and the SNO Chorus. Folk, Rhythm &
Blues and Country & Western music can be heard in a variety of pubs

and clubs throughout the city, and in June-July the city plays host to the annual Jazz and Folk Festivals which attract the world's top stars, and spill out from the official venues into various pubs and clubs till early in the morning. On the streets buskers provide entertainment for shoppers on an extraordinary variety of instruments from bagpipes to tin whistles and tenor saxophones. See THEATRES, **What's On**.

Necropolis: Overlooking Glasgow Cathedral, this graveyard was modelled on Pere Lachaise Cemetery in Paris and is packed with once-ornate (but now mostly crumbling) funereal monuments to wealthy Victorian Glaswegians. On top is a 18 m high Doric column (1825) commemorating the Protestant reformer John Knox (c.1513-1572). Castle St. 0800-2000 daily. Free.

Newspapers: Continental newspapers and magazines can be found at William Porteous, Newsagents and Booksellers, 9 Royal Exchange Place. Tel: 221 8623; John Smith & Son Ltd., 57 St Vincent St. (second floor). Tel: 221 7472; and in a kiosk in Buchanan St. just above the Underground Station. Only the *International Herald Tribune* and *USA Today* are widely available for American readers; these can be found in Central Station, the Buchanan St. kiosk, John Menzies and W. H. Smith in Argyle St. pedestrian precinct.
The main Glasgow newspapers are the *Glasgow Herald*, *Daily Record* and the *Evening Times* which provide a lively commentary on city affairs and entertainments. There are also numerous free sheets available of varying quality such as *The Glaswegian*, and *Glasgow Guardian*. Other Scottish papers include: *The Scotsman*; *Sunday Mail*; and *Sunday Post. See* **What's On**.

Nightlife: Glasgow offers a wide range of entertainment and cultural pursuits, including live theatre - from experimental drama to popular comedy; the latest cinema releases; or live music in the evening ranging from classical and opera to folk and jazz or alternative bands at the Barrowland. For the energetic there are the city's lively discos and nightclubs (some offering traditional ceilidh nights and Scottish dancing). In addition to the wide choice of restaurants and fashionable bar/diners in and around the city, you can forsake the shore for a romantic candlelit dinner cruise on the Clyde. An evening in a traditional city pub should equip you with all you need to know about local customs and 'patter', and there are always the more fashionable pubs and wine bars for those who prefer not to stand at a bar for three hours drinking pints and discussing football. For those born lucky there are three casinos dotted about the centre. See NIGHTLIFE, PUBS, RESTAURANTS, THEATRES, **Tourist Information**.

Opening Times: Business hours are normally 0930-1730. Shops open 0900-1700 daily except Sunday, although Sunday opening and late opening on certain weekdays (usually Thursday) has become more common in recent years. Newsagents, bakeries, etc., will open earlier. Some shops in outlying areas may close on Tuesday afternoons. Banks open 0930-1530 Mon.-Fri., with extended hours on certain days. Post Offices open 0900-1730 Mon.-Fri., 0900-1300 Sat. Many pubs are open all day 1100-2300 Mon.-Sat., 1230-1430, 1830-2300 Sun., and often later during the Mayfest, Jazz and Folk Festivals in the summer months. Off-licenses open 0900-2200 Mon.-Sat.

Orientation: The city-centre streets form a grid with Sauchiehall St. and Argyle St. marking the northern and southern boundaries, and the High St. and M8 motorway at Charing Cross forming the eastern and western extremes of the central area. Most of the city streets run horizontally  and vertically within these limits, many of them radiating outwards from George Square. The city is divided by the River Clyde and the north-south divisions are linked by road and rail bridges, the Clyde Tunnel and the Underground Railway system.

Parking: See **Driving**.

Passports and Customs: A valid passport is required to enter Britain; citizens of the USA, Commonwealth, European and South American countries do not require a visa. Health certificates are not required unless one arrives from Asia, Africa or South America. There are no passport or customs formalities when entering Scotland from other areas of Britain. See **Duty Free**.

People's Palace: Three floors of exhibits concentrating on the social and economic history of Glasgow from early medieval times to the present day. The emphasis is on the lives and perspectives of ordinary people, and this fascinating collection covers trade and industry, religion, the Temperance Movement, trade unionism, arts and entertainment, sport and famous personalities. See ART & CULTURE, **Glasgow Green.**

Petrol: Petrol is sold in three grades: 4 Star at 38.2p per litre, 3 Star at 38p per litre and 2 Star (for vans) at 37.8p per litre. Unleaded petrol is

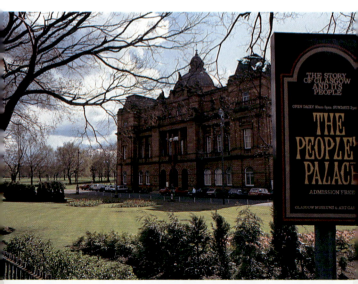

widely available at 36.9p per litre as is diesel at 34p per litre. Most petrol stations are self-service and the instructions on the pumps are easy to follow. 24-hour petrol stations: Marlborough Filling Station, 890 Pollokshaws Rd; St George's, 147 St George's Rd; Swan National, The Boating Pond, 1057 Great Western Rd; Universal Garage, 367 Alexandra Parade.

Pets: Animals brought into the UK must be placed in quarantine for six months as a precaution against rabies.

Police: Policemen and women wear black uniforms and a flat cap with a chequered band, and should be easy to find if you need one; as well as patrolling on foot they can often be seen riding through the streets of the city centre on horseback. Glasgow 'A' Division, Stewart St. Tel: 332 1113; Strathclyde Police Headquarters, 173 Pitt St. Tel: 204 2626. See **Crime and Theft, Emergencies**.

Post Offices: Post Boxes are red. A first class stamp (next day delivery) is 20p, second class (delivery within five days) is 15p. Air mail to the USA is 34p, Europe 24p, Australia and New Zealand 37p. All aerogrammes are 30p.
Letters sent to you 'Poste Restante' to the main post office will be kept for three months then returned to the sender. As well as stamps, Post Offices provide other services including currency exchange, Phonecards, postcards and stationery.
Head Post Office: George Square. Tel: 248 2882.
Branch Offices:
Charing Cross, 533 Sauchiehall St. Tel: 221 5529.
Dixon St. Tel: 248 6736.
Gorbals, 6/8 Cumberland Arcade. Tel: 429 6351.
Hope St., 216 Hope St. Tel: 332 4598.
St Rollox, 18 Glebe St. Tel: 552 4674.
See **Opening Times**.

Princes Square: A stylish shopping mall in the heart of the city, converted from historic buildings dating from 1841, with cafés, bars,

restaurants, upmarket boutiques found nowhere else in Scotland, and a programme of daily entertainment including music, dance and comedy during the summer. It also has a Foucault Pendulum which uses the rotation of the earth to tell the time of day, decorative mosaics, fountains and etchings. See **SHOPPING 2**.

Provand's Lordship: The oldest surviving house in Glasgow. Founded in 1471 by Bishop Andrew Muirhead as part of the nearby St Nicholas Hospital, it served as the city residence of the Prebend - or Provand - of Barlanark, an official of the Cathedral. Mary Queen of Scots may have stayed here in 1566 when her husband Lord Darnley lay sick in a house near by. It has passed through many uses (including alehouse and sweet shop) and is now a museum with antique furniture, tapestries, paintings and various other exhibits of historical interest, including a reconstruction of the chamber of Cuthbert Simson, Clerk to the Cathedral Chapter (1501-13), using contemporary furnishings and artefacts. 3-7 Castle St. 1000-1700 Mon.-Sat., 1400-1700 Sun. Free.

Provan Hall: A two-storey 16thC house with crow-stepped gables and round tower (with 18thC additions). It was originally the country

residence of the Prebend of Barlanark (see previous entry) and is one of
the few surviving buildings from medieval Glasgow. It is now used as a
community centre. Auchinlea Park, Garthamlock (at the Auchinlea
Road entrance), north east of the city off the M8.

Public Holidays: New Year's Day - 1 January - is the only statutory
public holiday. On Bank Holidays many shops and businesses also
close for all or part of the day: 2 January, Friday before Easter, first and
last Monday in May, first Monday in August, 30 November (St
Andrew's Day), 25 and 26 December.

Public Toilets: Toilets in hotels, restaurants and cafés are usually
clean and pleasant as are those in the large shopping centres such as
Princes Square; in some older pubs the facilities are less adequate.
Public conveniences in the city centre also vary in quality. Central
Station and Queen Street Station offer the most comprehensive facilities
including showers and shaving sockets.

Rabies: See **Pets**.

Radio and Television: The BBC operates two national television
stations - BBC1 and BBC2 - and four national radio stations, including
BBC Radio Scotland. The IBA provides regional television services -
STV in Scotland - and Channel 4.
Television: BBC1 (Scotland): light entertainment, news, sport. BBC2:
Drama, documentaries, music and the arts. STV: light entertainment,
sport and current affairs.
Channel 4: Arts and culture, news, documentaries and minority pro-
grammes.
Radio: BBC Radio Scotland (370m/810 Hz): news, information, drama.
Radio Clyde (261m VHF 102.5): Music, chat shows, news and traffic
information.
For programme details see *Radio Times* (all BBC Radio and TV) and the
TV Times (STV, Channel 4 and Radio Clyde) available in newsagents.

Railways: Services to the south side of the city, south-west Scotland

GLASGOW · *European City of Culture, 1990*

AWAEYEGOYAMUGYE

and the Clyde resorts; and to London (up to five trains a day to
Euston), the Midlands, Wales and the west of England run from
Central Station in Gordon St.
Queen Street Station provides services to the north of the city, the
north and east of Scotland (half hourly to Edinburgh); the scenic West
Highland route to Oban, Fort William and Mallaig; and the eastern
route to London (via York and Newcastle).
There is a shuttle bus service every 15 min. between Central and
Queen Street Stations 0800-1900 Mon.-Sat.
For all British Rail enquiries, tel: 204 2844; Sleeper Reservations, tel:
221 2305 (Central), 332 9811 (Queen St.).

Religious Services:
Church of Scotland: Glasgow Cathedral, Castle St.;
Renfield St Stephen's Church, 262 Bath St.
Baptist: Adelaide Place Church, 209 Bath St.
Congregational: Hillhead Centre, 1 University Avenue.
Episcopal Church of Scotland: Cathedral Church of St Mary, 300 Great
Western Road.
Roman Catholic: St Andrews Cathedral, 90 Dunlop St.
Central Mosque Islamic Centre, Adelphi St.
Jewish Orthodox: Garnethill Synagogue, 29 Garnet St.
Methodist: Woodlands Church, 229 Woodlands Road.
Greek Orthodox: St Luke's, 27 Dundonald Road.
For details of services contact the Tourist Information Centre
35-39 St Vincent Place. Tel: 227 4880.

Restaurants: See RESTAURANTS, Eating Out.

Sauchiehall Street: The name means 'willow meadow', but the
willow trees have long since gone and the street is now one of the main
shopping areas in the city, and also features the Willow Tearooms (see
MACKINTOSH), the McLellan Galleries (see **A-Z**) and Third Eye Centre
(see **ART & CULTURE**). See **WALK 2**.

Scottish Exhibition and Conference Centre: A 64-acre site on the north bank of the Clyde, the second-largest exhibition complex in Britain. Off the Clydeside Expressway. Tel: 204 2161. See **NIGHTLIFE**.

Shopping: Glasgow is Britain's third-largest shopping centre after London and Birmingham. The main shopping areas in the city are Argyle St., Sauchiehall St. and Buchanan St. (all of which are partly pedestrianized), and all the major chain stores are represented. Lewis's in Argyle St. is the largest department store in Scotland, and other large department stores are Arnotts in Argyle St. and Frasers in Buchanan St. The recently opened St Enoch Centre is a £62 million glass-covered shopping complex incorporating 50 shop units, fast-food court, ice-rink and multi-storey car park. A new £70 million shopping complex adjoining the new concert hall is also planned to open in 1990 in

Sauchiehall St., which already has its own indoor shopping centre. Other covered shopping areas include Princes Square and the Argyll Arcade, both in Buchanan St. The Merchant City has recently developed into a fashionable area, and boasts some stylish boutiques selling designer clothing and interior decor; Candleriggs Market; and the new Italian Centre also planned to open in 1990. For real bargains 'The Barras', Glasgow's famous street market in the Gallowgate, is the place to visit at weekends. See **SHOPPING**.

Smith, Madeleine (1835-1928): Suspect in a sensational murder case, who lived at 7 Blythswood Square. She stood trial in Edinburgh in 1857 for the suspected murder by arsenic poisoning of her lover Pierre Emile L'Angelier. Her explicit love letters shocked contemporary Victorian sensibilities and generated considerable public hostility towards her. She needed L'Angelier out of the way so she could become engaged to a wealthier and more acceptable suitor, and she did buy arsenic on three occasions. However the date on a crucial love letter was illegible, her lawyer put up a brilliant defence and a verdict of 'Not Proven' was returned. Eventually she emigrated to America where she remained until her death, despite threats to deport her for refusing to appear in a proposed Hollywood film biography.

Smoking: Now banned on the Underground and increasingly restricted on other forms of public transport, in many theatres, cinemas, restaurants and in other public places. See **Cigarettes and Tobacco**.

Souvenirs: See **SHOPPING 1**, **Best Buys**.

Sports: Football is Glasgow's largest spectator sport and the rivalry between the city's local teams Rangers and Celtic (the 'Old Firm') is world famous. The Kelvin Hall Sports and Recreation Complex has an international-standard athletics track plus two sports halls with room for 1500 spectators. In 1990 it plays host to the European Indoor International, the premier athletic event of the year. For horse-racing enthusiasts there is a course at Hamilton (11 km from Glasgow) and at Whitletts Road in Ayr (60 km south of the city). Greyhound racing and

The tree refers to a frozen branch miraculously kindled into flame by Mungo when the fire went out at his school in Culross. The bird is his teacher's pet robin which he restored to life after cruel boys had killed it. The fish refers to the tale of the queen of Strathclyde who gave her ring to her warrior lover; the king discovered the ring and threw it into the river. The queen, threatened with death by her husband if she could not produce the ring, begged Mungo for help. He told her to send a fisherman to cast his line into the water, a salmon was caught, and in its mouth was the vital ring. The bell refers to a holy bell which Mungo supposedly brought from Rome; on returning he gave a speech of thanksgiving saying 'Let Glasgow flourish by the preaching of Thy Word and the praising of Thy Name' - which is the city's motto.

Stock Exchange: An example of Gothic Venetian design by John Burnet (1875). The building now houses modern offices and is not open to the public, but the Stock Exchange on the first floor of the extension does have a Visitor's Gallery. Nelson Mandela Place. 1000-1245, 1400-1530 Mon.-Fri.

Students: Foreign students with an International Student Card can travel at reduced cost on public transport. Contact St Enoch Travel Centre for details. Tel: 226 4826.

Taxis: Familiar black cabs with yellow 'For Hire' light on the roof. City Centre taxi ranks: Central Station (Gordon St.); North Hanover Street (off George Sq.). West End rank: Queen Margaret Drive on the

corner of Great Western Rd.
Taxi firms: Taxi Cab Association, 21 Lawmoor Rd. Tel: 332 6666;
TOA Taxis, 6a Lynedoch St. Tel: 332 7070/ 332 0103/554 7070.

Telephones and Telegrams: Public telephones are housed in per-spex booths (with yellow logo) and can also be found inside hotels, restaurants, bars, shops and garages. The minimum charge is 10p., some public phones only take plastic credit cards called Phonecards, purchased for £1, £2, £4 and £10 in post offices and shops displaying green Phonecard signs. The area code for Glasgow (041) should only be dialled when outside the city. Dial 100 for the operator; 192 for directory enquiries; 155 for the overseas operator; 999 for emergencies. International Direct Dialling: for Australia 01061; USA 0101; Canada 0101; New Zealand 01064.
Telemessages: Dial 100 and ask for Telemessage or International Telegrams. It operates for 24 hours daily, phone before 2200 Mon.-Sat. (1900 Sun.) for next day delivery.

Templeton's Business Centre: Built in 1889 for the famous carpet manufacturers William Templeton & Co., it was designed by William Leiper in the style of a Venetian palace to complement the natural surroundings (by order of the city council). Its ornate and multi-coloured glazed brickwork make it one of the most dazzling and intriguing buildings in the city. See **Glasgow Green**.

Tenement House Museum: A typical red sandstone tenement building in Garnethill dating from 1892, restored by the National Trust for Scotland and opened as a museum. The hall, parlour, bedroom, kitchen and bathroom are filled with contemporary furnishings, cast-iron kitchen range and gas lighting. See ART & CULTURE, WALK 2.

Time Differences: Scotland, like the rest of Britain, observes Greenwich Mean Time, which is five hours ahead of Standard Eastern Time. March to October is British Summer Time, which is GMT plus one hour. Glasgow 1200 is New York 0700; Sydney 2100; Auckland 2300; Jo'burg 1300.

Tipping: There is no general rule about tipping; waiters, hotel staff, hairdressers and taxi drivers will expect a small sum; in restaurants 10% is not unusual if the meal has been enjoyable, even where service has been included.

Tobacco Lords: In the 1770s Glasgow was importing over half of all tobacco brought into Britain and most of it was re-exported to Europe. The merchants involved in this trade - men like John Glassford (1715-83), Alexander Speirs (1714-82), and William Cunninghame (d. 1789) - became wealthy and powerful figures who dominated the social and economic life of the city. They would meet in the Trongate to discuss business and display their red cloaks, satin breeches and powdered wigs. Of the great mansions which they built for themselves, only Cunninghame's survives, now the main section of Stirling's Library in Royal Exchange Square (see **WALK 1**, **A-Z**).

Tolbooth Steeple: This seven-storey steeple at Glasgow Cross is all

that remains of the 17thC Tolbooth (or Town House) which served as a courthouse, jail and town hall. See **Glasgow Cross**.

Tourist Information: Greater Glasgow Tourist Board, Tourist Information Centre 35-39 St Vincent Place. 0900-1800 Oct.-March, Mon.-Sat.; 0900-2100 Apr.-Sept., Mon.-Sat., 1000-1800 Sun. Tel: 227 4880.

Tours: Strathclyde Buses run a City Bus Tour from St Enoch Square daily from 28 April-26 September at 1400; also 27 June-12 August Mon.-Fri. at 1015; adults £3, children/concessions £2; pay the driver. There is also a special tour of Mackintosh buildings during the summer including tea at Queen's Cross Church, contact the Travel Centre, St Enoch Square for details. Taxi tours of the city are available (one to five persons): a two-hour tour around the centre and east of the city (£17 per taxi), and a three-hour tour including the Burrell Collection (£24). Contact the Taxi Cab Association. Tel: 332 6666.
Chauffeur driven/guided tours are also avilable, contact: Glasgow Chauffeur Drive, 15 Woodrow Rd. Tel: 427 6622. Little's Chauffeur

Drive, 1282 Paisley Road West. Tel: 883 2111. H. Winchole, 214-218 Howard St. Tel: 552 0251. For tours arranged to suit individual require- ments contact: See Scotland, 17 Dalziel Drive. Tel: 427 0777. See **Guides**, **Tourist Information**.

Trades House: Headquarters of 14 incorporated trades of Glasgow (now mainly charitable organizations). Designed by Robert Adam in 1794, the facade remains largely intact (the interior was remodelled by James Sellars, 1887-88). Inside the mahogany-panelled banqueting hall is a 19thC frieze depicting the various trades at work.
85 Glassford St. 1000-1700 Mon.-Fri. Free.

Transport: For all underground, bus, rail, and ferry information in the Strathclyde region contact the Travel Centre, St Enoch Sq 0900-1700 Mon.-Sat. Tel: 226 4826. See **Buses, Railways, Underground.**

Transport Museum: A wonderful collection on two floors of vin- tage cars, motorbikes and bicycles (including the oldest in the world), old Glasgow trams, horse-drawn carriages, railway locomotives and other transport. There is also a recreation of a typical suburban Glasgow street from the 1930s, and the Clyde Room containing 600 model ships reflecting the history and importance of the Clyde in shipbuilding and marine engineering. See **CHILDREN.**

Traveller's Cheques: See **Money**.

Tron Steeple: All that remains of the old Tron Church (1637) burnt down in the late 18thC by a gang of rowdies on horseback who called themselves the 'Hellfire Club'. The new church building now houses the Tron Theatre. See **THEATRES.**

Underground: 0630-2240 Mon.-Sat. Reduced service Sun., hols. 40p. The cheapest and easiest way of travelling in the city. Trains run every four to six minutes (evenings eight minutes) between 15 stations. There are interchanges with the suburban train line at Partick and at Buchanan Street (via a moving walkway to Queen Street Station). You

can purchase a Strathclyde Transport Transcard allowing unlimited travel on Underground, trains and Strathclyde Buses at St Enoch Station (Inner Area: £6 per week). You will need a passport-sized photograph (photo booths in the station).

University of Glasgow: Established by Bishop Turnbull in 1451, Glasgow is the second oldest university in Scotland after St Andrews. Originally situated in the High St. near the Cathedral, the 17thC Old College was demolished in 1870 when the university moved to Sir George Gilbert Scott's flamboyant Gothic-style building (1866-70) on Gilmorehill. The impressive tower and openwork spire was added by the architect's son J. Oldrid Scott in 1888 and rises to over 91 m (tel: 339 8855 ext 4271 to arrange a climb to the top). The university has over 10,000 students and enjoys an impressive reputation in the arts, sciences and medicine. **U** Hillhead. See **WALK 3**.

University of Strathclyde: Established in 1964, Strathclyde was formerly the Royal College of Science and Technology, and before that Anderson's College, a technical institution dating back to 1775. The University has over 7000 students, many of them from overseas, and incorporates the Strathclyde Business School, one of the largest in Europe. North east of George Square. See **WALK 1**.

Watt, James (1736-1819): Civil engineer born in Greenock. At the age of 18 he became apprenticed to a Glasgow mathematical instrument maker. At this time, accurate instruments were in great demand, and in 1760 he was appointed instrument maker to the University and had a workshop in the Trongate. His outstanding achievement was to perfect the design of the Newcomen steam engine (the idea supposedly came to him while out walking on Glasgow Green in 1765) which became the workhorse of the Industrial Revolution. He retired in 1800 and died in Birmingham at the age of 83. Some of the tools from his workshop can be seen in the Hunterian Museum at Glasgow University (see **ART & CULTURE**).

What's On: There are several guides to cinemas, theatres, music,

exhibitions and sporting events in the city. All are available in newsagents:

The List, a fortnightly guide for Glasgow and Edinburgh.

What's On, issued free monthly. Other free sheets like *Culture City* are distributed in pubs, cafés and public venues throughout the city.

Dial 248 4000 for events in Greater Glasgow each week. Daily newspapers provide similar information; particularly useful are the *Glasgow Herald* and *Evening Times*. The Tourist Information Centre in St Vincent Place provides comprehensive details for all venues and events in the city. **See Newspapers**, **Tourist Information**.

Youth Hostels: Scottish Youth Hostels Association, Glasgow District Office, 12 Renfield St. Tel: 226 3976.

Glasgow Youth Hostel, 11 Woodlands Terrace. Tel: 332 3004.

Grade 1, 120 beds, £4.25 per night. Self catering facilities.